Sleeping in the Bathtub

KIMBERLI
ROESSING-ANDERSON

DEDICATION

For Kaila and Ryan

CONTENTS

ACKNOWLEDGMENTS

The Aull House.

The Charleston Gazette-Mail

Davidson, Kenneth T.

The Dominion Post

The Monongalia Public Records Department

The Record Delta

Ricker, Judy

Trans-Allegheny Lunatic Asylum Historical Tours

The West Virginia Supreme Court Archives

Thank you to my family.

INTRODUCTION

Walking quickly but trying to look calm. Hands stuffed deep into his denim jacket pockets. One hand still holding the gun. The gun was hot. One foot in front of the other looking straight ahead, he walked. The smell of smoke filled his nose. There was sweat on his brow and under his nostrils, make his mustache itch. His legs felt like cement. His ears rang from the blasts. The wind caught his strawberry-blonde hair and startled him. His stomach turned over and over as he could hear yelling behind him on the Stadium Bridge. He did not dare look back. As he got closer to his downstairs apartment, he could hear sirens. Once he could see his house, his heart began to beat wildly. He walked inside and slammed the door behind him. Safe.

1

Now his legs were weak like jello. His hands shook as he removed the gun from his pocket and set it on a table. He adjusted his glasses. He took off his hat and jacket and laid them on a chair. He had made it home but how long would it be before the police found him? Shooting three men would not go unpunished. He went to his window as he so often did and watched. He rubbed his beard and listened until the sirens stopped, the yelling ceased, and the town returned to relative quiet. Exhausted, he went to the bathroom and climbed into the bathtub. He drifted off to sleep.

While Tim was walking home, the scene near the Stadium Bridge had erupted into chaos. People heard gunfire and emptied out of the surrounding bars in Sunny Side (near Morgantown, West Virginia). Traffic stopped, and people got out to tend to the wounded. Three men lay in the immediate area with gunshot wounds to their torsos. Bystanders compressed their wounds and tried to keep the three young men awake. Someone called the police. There was yelling. The victims cried out in agony. The bystanders tried to comfort them and keep them calm. Blood ran onto the street and stained both the victim's clothes and those working to aid them. Someone stuffed a pink doonnat into one man's wound to try and stop the bleeding. It was madness at midnight.

One victim died. For all the attempts to save him, he bled out and died shortly after arriving at the hospital. He was barely alive when the ambulance swung open its doors and pulled him out. His eyes were starting to dilate. His vital signs were falling. Doctors and nurses worked on him feverishly, but he died. Two more ambulances arrived with young men being whisked away into the emergency department. Doctors initially believed that one of the victims had been shot multiple times. A mere tricked played by the damage of a hollow point bullet. Both men were rushed into surgery where surgeons tried to undo the damage that had been done by Timothy Allen McWilliams, that night. The two victims survived but endured extended hospital stays, surgeries, and pain.

1 TIM

I met Timothy Allen McWilliams several times during 1987 and 1988. I was dating and briefly engaged to his youngest brother, Jeff. Tim was quiet. He shuffled when he walked and was bent over like an elderly man twice his age. His hair was dark and unkept. He seemed to always have the beginnings of a beard. Tim didn't make eye contact with me, but he would say, "Hi Kim" or "How are you, Kim?". He would reply to direct questions that only required yes or no answers. He spoke mostly at the behest of his parents (Leo and Ginny). They would coax him like a toddler just learning vocabulary words. His plaid shirts and jeans hung on his frame. I could see the outline of his collarbone. His affect was flat. Tim's foot was always tapping under the kitchen table.

4

This was caused by a condition known as Akathisia. Akathisia is a state of agitation, distress, and restlessness that is an occasional side-effect of antipsychotic and antidepressant drugs (Delisi, 2017). Tim also lost skin on his feet from rocking back and forth from this same condition.

Country music would play quietly in the background from a small radio in the kitchen. A Feral black cat that only liked Leo would curl around the back of his neck on a counter behind the kitchen table. The doors would be open for ventilation. Ginny would cook, and we would all eat and then clear the table. Tim ate, but not a lot as I remember. Tim helped clean up and whatever his parents asked him to do, but it was robotic. He didn't seem to have much original thought or movement.

Compared to his senior picture, he was a shadow of his former self. The image was of a young man that was confident and going places with his life. He looked athletic and was handsome. It was hard to believe it was the same guy. We played cards together with Leo and other family members. Games of Hearts and Spades were the favorites. We watched football. I am not sure if I ever saw Tim smile.

Tim looked off into space a lot. It was as if he was daydreaming. He did yard work with Leo. He followed Leo around like a shadow in and out of the small white house on Victoria Street. Tim helped take care of the English Bulldogs the family raised and bred. Tim seemed passive.

At night, I would lie wide awake in the dark in a back bedroom of that house, as Tim rocked back and forth in a rocking chair in his attic bedroom. This rocking was also a side effect of his medication for schizophrenia. I did not know that then. What I knew was that Tim has shot three people in 1980 at WVU (West Virginia University) and that one of them had died. I knew that Tim had been living at Weston State Hospital before being released to his parents. The family didn't tell me about Tim even though I had been dating Jeff for a long time. I stumbled across the court documents and newspaper clippings while looking for typing paper in the back bedroom one weekend. I was stunned that no one had told me.

Although Tim never touched me or threatened me in any way; I was afraid of him. I was not able to sleep when we visited their home in Buckhannon. Tim's mere demeanor frightened me and more so at night. The house rested outside the city. The only light was the moon. The only sounds at night came from crickets, wildlife, and Tim rocking back and forth in a rocking chair in the attic. My imagination often ran wild on those nights, and I was genuinely afraid of Tim. I always thought Tim would kill again. I was surprised it took thirty years for it to happen.

2 AND THEN THERE WERE FOUR

In January of 1953, Norman Leonard McWilliams (from Grafton, WV) and Virginia Bosley McWilliams (from Marion, WV) welcomed the first of four blonde babies into the world. Leo and Ginny were only about twenty-years-old and had been married roughly a year. From 1953 through 1966, three boys and one girl would be born: Timothy Allen (1953), Rita Mae in (1955), Mark Dwayne in (1961), and Jeffrey Lynn (1966). One plump blonde baby after the next was born and raised by Leo and Ginny who lived first in Clarksburg, WV and then in a rural area near Buckhannon, West Virginia. All four children were healthy, attractive, and smart. They spent summers working and playing on farms. They camped, fished, and hunted. All four played sports and did well in school. They were all excellent swimmers.

I remember Ginny talking about Tim often. Tim was very bright. He could read when was just three-years-old. He had a genius IQ. Tim had been a star athlete. He was captain of the football team and on the Homecoming Court. He was one of two escorts for the Queens of the Strawberry Festival (a famous festival in Buckhannon, West Virginia). His senior picture hung proudly on the wall behind the couch. Tim had a near perfect ACT score. Tim read the dictionary as a kid and the encyclopedia (when we still had encyclopedias). Ginny seemed quite proud of him.

Ginny bragged about him often and more than any of the other children. I thought it was sweet. I knew he was a Marine. I knew that he had enlisted during the 1970's. I had seen a picture of him in uniform and another with his girlfriend (Judy). However, no one ever talked about Tim (in the present). I was afraid he had died. Jeff told me that he was alive, but no other details. I figured that (like Mark) Tim lived in Florida. I had never met Mark either. I didn't think too much of it. Maybe, I should have.

In reality, Tim had been a wonderful child by all accounts. Born on January 29, 1953, he spent about twelve years of his childhood in Clarksburg and then the family moved to Buckhannon as Leo changed jobs. Tim had many friends, and they would congregate at his house. Ginny testified at trial that Tim's friends would seem to show up at dinner time. The kids spent time during the summers at their cousin's farm. Leo took them camping. Tim was an athlete. Leo signed him up to play football as a child. Tim excelled at school, and according to the testimony of both of his parents, he was trusted and well-behaved. Leo stated that Tim was responsible and they didn't have to worry about him. He would wait up for the other kids to come home at night and lock-up the house according to his father's testimony.

By the time Tim was a senior in high school, the world seemed to be his oyster. He was a handsome young man with girlfriends and good grades. He was co-captain of the football team and on the homecoming court at Buckhannon Upshur High School. His 1971 yearbook is filled with photos of him in different activities and notes from well-wishers. The autographs from classmates overran the signing pages and spread onto the pages of pictures. He was popular. Tim could have gone straight to college, but he decided to join the Marines instead. He wanted to earn some money so the burden would not be on his parents to pay for his college expenses.

Flanked by references, he signed up for the Marine Corps on March 11, 1971. Tim trained at Parris Island in South Carolina, and he was first stationed at Camp LeJeune, North Carolina. Tim was interested in being an equipment mechanic according to his intake form. He signed up for four years of active duty and two years of reserves for a total of six years. Tim's intake form listed his physical condition as excellent. Tim was 5 foot 7 inches, blonde hair and blue eyes. He's listed himself as a Methodist. His enlistment began on August 31, 1971.

He completed his training and was then stationed in North Carolina where he would come back to Buckhannon and visit his family on weekends and holidays. By this time, Rita had married and started her own family, and Tim liked to visit her. Tim and Rita's husband liked to go hunting together. Back at base, he earned medals of good conduct and marksmanship while in the Marine Corps. According to his weapons firing record, he was trained on a .45 pistol, M-14, .38 pistol, riot gun, and a shotgun. According to his military records, he had awards for his shooting ability. Tim was comfortable handling firearms.

At some point, Tim became bored with Camp Lejeune, North Carolina and wanted to do something different. He decided he wanted to be a member of the prestigious embassy guard. Tim wanted to see more of the world. He was again flanked by references in and out of the military. He went to embassy school. By 1973, he was on his way to Riyadh in Saudi Arabia. This was a dangerous assignment. The assignment came with top security clearance and conditions. Tim had to agree to remain unmarried until the end of his duty. His visits to Buckhannon stopped as well. For the next two years, he served in both Riyadh, Saudi Arabia and Tunis, Tunisia as an embassy guard. His family didn't see him for two years.

On the surface, it appeared that Tim had a successful military career. He was promoted to Lance Corporal, and he was again promoted to Sergeant. He had commendations: A

National Defense Service Medal, Good Conduct Medals, and a Meritorious Unit Commendation. Aside from a speeding ticket in 1972 in Jacksonville, North Carolina, he didn't have a smudge on his military record. Before entering embassy guard school, he had accumulated 375 hours as an equipment mechanic. Moving from the Department of Defense to the State Department as an embassy guard was also seen as a promotion. He received top secret clearance. Tim received positive reviews from his commanders. In 1972, one stated, *"Lance Corporal McWilliams was interviewed on 26 December 1972 and presented a very favorable impression. His appearance was outstanding, and he displayed a mature and self-confident attitude. He is considered a suitable applicant for assignment with the Department of State's Foreign Service Establishment overseas."*

Tim first served at the embassy in Riyadh, Saudi Arabia. He was only there a year, but his time there would affect him long afterwards. He would tell various doctors and even police that he was not comfortable around Arabs. Tim was upset when a student from Egypt moved-in near his apartment in Morgantown. He believed that this host country of Saudi

Arabia had been involved in sodomy. Many of Tim's delusions centered around events that happened in Riyadh and Tim would tell doctors that he had memories of people being killed at that embassy. He also told Rita about those flashbacks.

3 JUDY JUDY JUDY

While in Tunis, Tunisia, Tim began dating a woman named Judy Ricker. She was from Seattle, Washington. Judy had been studying in Paris when she took a spring break vacation to see her sister (Anne) who was in Tunisia. During an interview with Judy, she told me that she liked it there and it was warmer than Paris. She decided to stay. Judy met Tim at a party at the Marine House. Tim had been stationed in Riyadh and recently transferred to Tunis, Tunisia. Judy described him as tan and very handsome. *"He was in fabulous shape."*

Tim was a runner. He was an athletic, bright, funny and a nice guy. Tim cared about how he appeared and that he knew he was nice-looking. Judy described Tim as a focused young person. *He was very controlled in his emotions. He was confident.* They met in 1973. They dated for about 1 ½ years. She worked for a publisher as a French translator and then for University of South Carolina Geological Department.

He officially lived at the Marine House, but he also shared apartments with Judy in Sidi Bou Said and Tunis. Tim had a self-deprecating sense of humor according to Judy, but he could have a temper (especially if he drank). Tim and Judy were very happy there. They had two cats (Butch and Madame Maquillage (which means made up in French because she had black markings around her eyes that looked like they were made-up). Judy remembers these as good times.

She and Tim discussed marriage, and she even spent a summer visiting Tim's family in Buckhannon, WV. However, Judy did not want to live in Morgantown, WV for four years while Tim went to college. She wanted to be closer to her family out west, Judy moved on to California after Tim was discharged. They tried dating long distance. It didn't work very well even though Judy visited Tim a couple of times at school. They remained friends and wrote letters to each other. She first noticed a change in Tim during his second year at WVU. She said he spoke of conspiracies theories often. Judy also stated that Tim thought he was being followed. *The changes were gradual. He had become quite paranoid.* Judy did not know Tim to have guns other than a hunting rifle. Judy stated that Tim did like to go hunting. She thought that the only reason that Tim bought the other guns at WVU was because he was afraid of something.

Judy stated that she was never contacted by the prosecution nor the defense for either of Tim's trials in 1984. She said she would have been willing to testify. Judy also did not know that his case had been overturned by the West Virginia Supreme Court in 1986. Judy wanted people to know that before Tim became ill, he was a sweet guy. *He was a kind individual that (in his right mind) would never want to hurt anyone.* Judy did not believe that the government had given Tim any experimental drug to make him forget government secrets or documents. Judy thought Tim had become mentally ill and that he was delusional. Judy had not spoken to Tim since before the shootings in 1980. She remembered Tim's family as being the nicest people. She remembered Leo as being such a great guy and very funny. There was a sense of sadness in Judy's voice as our conversation ended. She was sad for everyone involved.

4 RITA

On some of my trips to Buckhannon, Rita was there. Rita was extroverted and funny. Everything stopped when she came into the room. She was cute and almost always fun to be around. After Leo and Ginny went to bed; we would often sit down and talk for hours just the three of us. I enjoyed that. During a conversation one night, Rita told me all about her eldest brother, Timothy Allen McWilliams, from her point of view. It was a story that made her laugh and made her cry. Her facial expressions were animated as were her hands. The lines in her face were creased when she was serious, and then her laugh lines would pop out as she threw her head back and giggled. This story of Tim's life was emotional for her.

Rita liked to make nachos. She would pour a massive bag of Doritos in a baking dish. She would cover them with a bag a of cheddar, a bag of mozzarella, a drained can of chili beans, and Jalapenos. She would microwave them, and they were delicious. Even though I was not twenty-one, we all sat, drank beer, and ate nachos. Rita told me many of the same things that Ginny had said about Tim, but from the viewpoint of the second child. She felt she was always compared to Tim. He was two years older. Rita explained that Tim was a perfect child. He never got into trouble, and he did as he was told. Rita didn't. She was wild and rebellious.

Rita was smart, but she didn't read at three-years-of-age. Rita was more street-smart. She was a little on the wild side. Yet, Rita and Tim were close. Rita looked up to Tim as they got older. He was an athlete and popular. Rita was coming into her own in high school as Tim was leaving it in 1971. She benefited from having an older/popular brother in school. She told us that Tim had had several girlfriends that he dated. One of those girls was a close friend of Rita's. He planned to go into the Marine Corps for four years and then attend West

Virginia University. Rita said that Tim was always a straight arrow.

Tim went into the Marines. Rita went on with life. Rita was then the eldest child at home, and she was a sixteen going on thirty. She could not wait to get out of the house and be on her own. Rita was married in her junior year of high school. Rita got married young, had two daughters by age 22, and was divorced in the blink of an eye. She was on her own. The granddaughters often visited Leo and Ginny, and I remember thinking how cute they were. When the girls would come over; Leo spoiled them rotten. They ran, played, and made those squealing noises little girls make. They swam in the above ground pool that Leo had built.

I had met both Mindy and Haley on several occasions. They were smiling and laughing little girls with blonde mops. They would play with the animals. They loved the Old English Bulldogs. They enjoyed being with their grandparents. They would play all day and then fall asleep during dinner. Leo would pick them up and carry them off to bed. Jeff loved them and stated that he wanted his first child to be named Jordan (after his hero-Michael Jordan). Rita talked about how much Tim loved those two little girls.

Rita explained that Tim had changed while he was overseas. Four years later, he looked different. His hair was darker, and he was withdrawn He wasn't the big strong, handsome Tim that Rita remembered. He was no longer carefree. His lust for life seemed gone. Rita thought it would just take some time for him to settle back into civilian life. He registered for school at WVU and moved to Morgantown. For two years, Tim did well, academically. This was expected as he graduated in the top 10% of his high school class and scored in the 97 percentile of the ACT. As he entered his third year of school, there was a change. At first, it was small things and comments he made about only eating specific food that would "regenerate" his brain.

I leaned in and listened. Rita explained that Tim was always afraid. She told us that Tim had begun sleeping in the bathtub that third year at WVU. He bought an extra- long phone extension cord so he could call her from the tub when he was afraid. He kept a gun with him at all times. He carried a gun on his person.

Rita had visited him (at WVU), and his apartment was a disaster of dirty dishes, filthy laundry and ammunition spread everywhere. Rita would try to clean-up. She would do the dishes and the laundry. She would pick-up his apartment. Tim's unusual behavior came way before people talked about PTSD (Post Traumatic Stress Disorder) Shell-Shock or other forms of mental illness associated with military service, out loud. Rita began to wonder what was wrong with her brother.

According to Webster's, Post-Traumatic Stress Disorder (PTSD) is trauma and stress-related disorder that may develop after exposure to an event or ordeal in which death, severe physical harm or violence occurred or was threatened. ... PTSD is frequently accompanied by depression, substance abuse, or anxiety disorders (Webster's, 2018). According to Webster's, Shell-shock is psychological disturbance caused by prolonged exposure to active warfare, especially being under bombardment (Webster's, 2018). Schizophrenia had not come into the picture in regards to Tim's behavior at that point.

The conversation about Tim spread over two nights. Rita was staying at the vacant house next door to her parents.

She had no heat, so she was only using a few of the rooms and had electric space heaters everywhere. I helped her paint the walls of the dining-room "hunter green" that weekend. Rita's humongous sheepdog was chained up outside the house pacing back and forth in front of the window on which I was working. The dog didn't seem to have a face. It was just a large dirty white hairball the size of a small elephant. Like her girls, the dog stayed at her parent's house. After dinner with the parents, we scooted across the yard to the all but empty house where Rita was living. Rita made nachos and cracked opened more beer. She continued the conversation about her brother.

Tim thought the government was after him by 1978. He believed that the government had given him an experimental drug to make him forget what he had seen in his final days at the embassy. Rita told us that Tim was a bodyguard for Henry Kissinger (I do not know if that is true). Tim was an important person at the embassy, and he saw secret documents that he wasn't supposed to see. Rita and Jeff seemed to both believe that the government had (in fact) given Tim an experimental drug. I wasn't so sure. Rita explained that Tim began drinking a lot and he may have been self-medicating with marijuana. He would tell Rita in these tortured bathtub conversations that he has was having flashbacks. He remembered bits and pieces of things he had seen while at the embassy. There were stories of dead women and children in black trash bags being carried by Tim and others through the embassy. Bags being dragged across marble floors leaving streaks of blood behind. He was afraid that if the government found out that he remembered these things; the CIA would kill him.

5 MARSHALL

At the time I dated Jeff, I was a staff writer for the school's (Marshall University, Home of the Thundering Herd and the subject of the film, "We Are Marshall") newspaper, "The Parthenon." Part of obtaining a journalism degree from the Marshall University School of Journalism was reporting for the Parthenon during freshman year. Some students stayed on as staff writers. I was one of those. I had access to a Reuters wire, an AP wire and other news outlets that I devoured. I was the kid that celebrated as much when CNN came to cable as when MTV came to cable. I was a news hound at about age twelve.

I love the news and politics. I watched CNN all the time growing up and then on my little black & white TV in my apartment at Marshall. I skipped classes at Marshall during the Iran/Contra Hearings. I was a real geek. After learning about Tim, I decided to go to the school library (something I rarely did) and look at both microfilm and in the stacks to find news articles about Timothy Allen McWilliams. I was surprised at how many stories there were. There were several between 1980-1984. There were a few more from 1986 when the West Virginia Supreme Court overturned Tim's conviction and acquitted him. This was a story. I had to look further. I needed to know more about Timothy Allen McWilliams. I wanted to understand how this seemingly docile man could have shot three people.

In the apartment, I shared with Jeff at Marshall University.

Jeff and I on the far left. 1987/88

Courtesy, Kenneth T. Davidson, 2018

6 WVU

My research indicated that Tim moved back to Buckhannon
after he was discharged from the Marines and immediately
enrolled at WVU as had always been his plan. Tim's family
went ahead to find him an apartment in Morgantown. They
rented the basement apartment at 44 Jones Ave. Tim lived
there all four years of college. Testimony from his family
members indicated that they found Tim to be a more serious
person when he came back from Tunisia and less likely to
chit-chat. Tim's family also stated that he seemed to be afraid
of something. He was always locking doors behind everyone
and warning them to do the same.

His basement apartment at 44 Jones Avenue was tucked
away in a cave of green plant life. Trees and shrubs stood in

every available spot. The red brick house poked out of the green background in photos presented at his two trials. A red and white awning offered shade. Tim was on the Sunnyside section of Morgantown. He was not far from campus. Tim had a porch and some plant-life veiled privacy. He had a truck for transportation. The luscious backyard would later be filled with frog traps and floodlights, but in the beginning, it was just green.

For two years at WVU, Tim seemed on the surface to do well. He had some issues with passing a class on surveying that he needed for his mining engineering degree, but he remained focused on graduating. I was able to look through some of the WVU yearbooks from 1977 and 1978 (courtesy of the Aull House next to the Morgantown Public Library), and I could not find Tim's picture anywhere which was in stark contrast to his high school yearbook where he appeared many times. Tim's main complaint by the summer of 1978, was that he was having a difficult time concentrating during a summer class and while doing his homework.

There were some other signs, however, that Tim was decompensating by 1978. He would visit Rita's family on the weekends instead of his parents. He confided in Rita that he thought his mother was poisoning his food. Around this time, Leo had cautioned Tim about carrying a gun on his person all the time. Tim would carry the gun in his pocket or leave it in the glove compartment of his vehicle. Tim would tell Rita about flashbacks he was having from the embassies. Tim was also developing a reputation of sorts at WVU in his neighborhood for being strange. He had placed two gigantic floodlights in his backyard that he turned them on at night. He trapped frogs. Tim had also called the police more than once because he thought there were prowlers in and around his basement apartment.

There was also the dog. On July 11, 1978, Tim pointed his shotgun from his apartment and shot into some bushes. He thought he had seen " human eyes" staring back at him (he would later tell his doctors). He ended up shooting a dog. Tim called the police indicating that someone had *"hit"* a dog and the police needed to come *"finish it off."* At the same time, the dog's owner (Jackie Flether) called the police because someone had shot her dog. Tim and Jackie were neighbors, and the dog had gotten loose. Morgantown Police

Report 803685 stated the following: After talking to the complainant, we spoke to Timothy A. McWilliams of 44 Jones Ave. McWilliams has had trouble with prowlers and heard a noise outside of his apartment. McWilliams took a 12-gauge shotgun out on his porch and yelled for the person to come out of the bushes. The person didn't emerge, and McWilliams fired at the bushes.

The person turned out to be a dog belonging to Jackie Flether of 35 ½ Jones Ave. McWilliams admitted to police that he shot the gun. A 12-gauge pump was lying on his couch and shells were positioned in various places throughout his apartment. The dog was not seriously wounded but did lose his tail. McWilliams was advised about the law on discharging firearms in the city and what would have happened if a person had been shot. They also advised the owner of the dog about what she could do. There was a note attached to the report: **Any officers responding to 44 Jones should use caution.** This was almost two years before the shooting outside Finnerty's Bar.

Type of Complaint _____ REQUEST POLICE

Location of Complaint ___35½ JONES AVE.___

Day __11__ Month __07__ Year __1978__ Time __0120__ AM PM EST PST

Received By ___DOMBEC___ (Phone) In Person Letter

Complainant (JACKIE PANTHER)

Address __35½ JONES AVE.___ Phone Number _____

Details of Complaint: SOMEONE JUST SHOT MY DOG NEED TO SEE A POLICEMAN

Officer Assigned: ___MACKEY - HESS___

Investigation Report: Date _____ Time _____ AM PM

Dog wounded by a shotgun while running loose.
Dog wounded very seriously. Talked to T. Walker @
McWilliamsΘ St. were dog was admitted at this same
day. _See Report #507454._

If additional space is needed use Form Number NPD - 1A. (DO NOT WRITE ON BACK)

Form Number: NPD - 1

Type of Complaint ___HURT ANIMAL___

Location of Complaint ___44 JONES AVE.___

Day __11__ Month ___07___ Year __1978__ Time __0119__ AM PM EST DST

Received By ___OGONES___

(Phone) In Person Letter

Complainant ___MAC WILLIAMS___

Address ___44 JONES AVE___ Phone Number _____

Details of Complaint: SOMEONE JUST HIT A DOG UPNEAR ON JONES AVE NEED AN OFFICER
TO FINISH THE DOG OFF.

Officer Assigned: ___MACKEY - REES___

Investigation Report: Date _____ Time _____ AM PM

After talking to (Complainant) at case # 907685
we talked to Timothy R. McWilliams at 44 Jones Ave.
McWilliams has had trouble with coyotes and heard
a noise outside in his yard went McWilliams took
a 12ga. shotgun out on his porch and waited for the
noise to come out of the bushes. The noise didn't
come out and McWilliams fired at the bushes. The
noise turned out to be a dog belonging to Jackie Fletcher
(she lives at 46 (sic) Jones). McWilliams admitted to
us that he shot the dog. 12ga. prop. buckshot so
his coat and clothes were painted in some places
throughout the garment.

If additional space is needed use Form Number IPD - 1A. (DO NOT WRITE ON BACK)

Form Number: IPD - 1   1864

34

COMPLAINT REPORT
JAMESTOWN POLICE DEPARTMENT

INVESTIGATION REPORT:

Date of this report _7-4-78_

Complaint Number _80,568_   Complainant _R.E. Williams_

DETAILS OF INVESTIGATION:

I advised R.E. Williams about the laws on discharging firearms in the City and that what it would have amounted to if a person had been shot. I also advised the owner of the dog what that she could do.

Also how others responding to this scene should use caution.

If more space is needed use Form Number 10D - 1A   (DO NOT WRITE ON BACK)

Tim only became worse after this incident. Tim later confided to doctors that he had also been shooting furniture within his apartment. He once shot his bed from near his bathroom because he thought there was someone after him. Looking at the photos from the search of his residence (after the shooting in 1980), it is the lodging of an unhinged man. The apartment was in complete disarray. Shotgun shells were everywhere on every available flat surface. There were tables with schoolbooks, a tape dispenser, and shotgun shells. There is a cabinet with plates, bananas and shotguns shells. There was a chest of drawers with magazines, pennies, and more shotgun shells. Tim was deeply afraid of something.

The carpet was un-vacuumed, jeans and shirts littered the furniture and floor. The apartment was dirty and unkept. Over 50 empty wine bottles lay on the floor and posters with instructions Tim wrote to himself were taped to the wall. The apartment was a mess and disorganized. It was (I think) a metaphor for Tim's mind. The location of items made no sense. Knives and guns were out and about. Shotgun shells were everywhere. Tim was sleeping in the bathtub. Any person who saw Tim's apartment would have had to realize that something was very wrong.

On one wooden flat surface (probably a table or desk) lay a box of nails, a map of Pittsburg, a rubber band, a key, several pairs of glasses, a book of 101 Famous Poems, a ruler, a gun holster, a red pencil, a political science textbook and several shotgun shells. On another brown wooden table lay a big blue & white box of cotton balls, shoe shining supplies, a toothbrush, lotion, what appears to be contacts and contact solution and more shotgun shells. Thick layers of dust covered everything. Yet, his bed was made up military style with a yellow wool blanket and bedspread.

As his behavior continued to deteriorate, Tim believed that the Communists were causing car crashes in the area. He believed they were responsible for the collapse of the Silver Bridge. The Silver Bridge was an eyebar chain suspension bridge built in 1928. It was named for the color of its aluminum paint. The bridge connected Point Pleasant, WV with Gallipolis, Ohio. It collapsed on December 15, 1967. The cause of the collapse was the failure of a single eyebar in the suspension chain. The bridge had been poorly maintained.

The bridge was full of rush-hour traffic. Forty-six people died. Two people were never found. This accident was the subject of the book and movie, The Mothman Prophecies (Wikipedia, 2018).

Tim also believed that Communists were responsible for the car bombing of a Morgantown Prosecutor in 1970. Joseph Laurita was severely injured in the bombing. He was at his home when he turned the ignition, and the car exploded. His wife was pregnant with their fourth child. Laurita was days away from going before a grand jury in a gambling case (Wikipedia, 2018). Tim also considered Communists responsible for the Marshall University plane crash on November 14, 1970, that killed 75 people including players, parents, and coaches. The plane crashed into a hillside two miles from Tri-State Airport (Wikipedia, 2018). The crash is the subject of the 2006 film; We Are Marshall. Tim also believed the Yablonski killings were perpetrated by Communists. On New Year's Eve, 1969, Joseph Yablonski (a labor leader from Pennsylvania) his wife, and daughter were shot to death at their home in Clarksville, PA (Wikipedia, 2018) Political opponents were responsible.

Tim said, "*this was all done through hypnosis because spies are trained in this.*" Tim would call Rita from his bathtub with these stories. Tim believed that he could not be shot by the government or the CIA if he was lying in his bathtub. The bathtub was bulletproof and some sort of safe zone where he could get some sleep. It was a place he where he could talk about his delusions with Rita. Tim had been terrified of the Jonestown Massacre that happened on November 17, 1978. Jim Jones was the American religious cult who initiated a mass suicide and murder in Jonestown, Guyana. He was the leader of the People's Temple. Over 900 people died (Wikipedia, 2018). Tim skipped three to four days of classes and would not leave his apartment.

Tim talked about eating special food that would regenerate his brain so that he would be smart again. He believed hormone therapy would increase his brain activity. Tim told doctors that donating plasma cleaned out his blood. Tim told Rita that he wanted to remember what happened in the embassy. He spoke of the government and CIA giving him a drug to make him forget about secret documents he had seen at the embassy. He also believed he was being brainwashed to go home to Buckhannon on the weekends. Tim thought he was going crazy because of the flashbacks. At trial, Tim would not discuss his delusions because of something he called, "The Official Secrets Act."

Tim was obsessed with numbers. He was obsessed with the numbers four and five. He felt it was an omen that he paid 444.00 dollars for the .45 gun a month before the shooting. The price was $325.00the gun and $7 for the hollow-point bullets. His address was 44 Jones Ave. The plasma center where he donated plasma (Sera Teach) had an address of 444.

Since the police made a note of the shotgun shells in 1978, and Rita spoke of the conditions of his apartment to me when I was dating Jeff, I am going to assume that Tim lived this way for at least a couple of years. Looking at the trial photos, it seems a far cry from how Tim would have lived in the Marine House in Tunisia or at the barracks in North Carolina as a Marine. This in combination with the phone calls that Rita described paint a picture of a very troubled two-year period for Tim leading up to the shootings in 1980.

7 RESEARCH

When I started researching this book, I made a trip to
Morgantown, WV (in May 2018) to view the case files which
I had obtained through the Freedom of Information Act
(FOIA) of West Virginia. I toured Weston State Hospital and
44 Jones Ave. where Tim had lived at the time of the crime.
Aside from a short weekend trip with my husband to see our
daughter, I had not been to Morgantown or Buckhannon in
many years. I had forgotten how steep the hills were and how
narrow the roads could be. Morgantown had changed
immensely. Where there was once very little, stores,
restaurants, and shops had taken over. It is a booming small
city and university town. There were three Starbucks in the
immediate vicinity. Places like Panda Express, Panera, and

Olive Garden lined the roads. Old red brick buildings and houses remained unchanged. It was odd.

The green luscious plant life was a welcomed site. As beautiful as Colorado is, it is never as green as West Virginia. Old Maple trees hung over us as we drove around the town. The flowers were bursting with color. I remembered the college, but not well. We found 44 Jones Ave. and of course, it looked nothing like the pictures from the trial. The plant life had been torn away in the back where Tim's apartment had been. The house was older and had white siding slapped over red brick is a vicious way. I took photos. The house was for rent, so I called the owner for a tour. It did not appear to be a great part of town but being close to the university; the place would probably still fetch high rent.

While in Morgantown, I would research all day at the Monongalia County Courthouse and then do my online research at night. I would make copies, but they were charging a dollar a page, so I took a lot of handwritten notes too. I took a few photos of items with my phone. I read about 4000 pages in a matter of days. At night I would transcribe my notes. My handwriting is not great, so that was a chore. There was a lot to take in on sites like Newspapers.com (Publisher's Edition) and Ancestry. I also used a background checking service. I was on about five databases while writing this book. I also took notes while visiting Weston State Hospital and touring 44 Jones Ave.

During my research, I could not believe the scope of the news articles on the 1980 arrest and the 1984 trials. The reporting was not at all in-line with what the family told me about Tim and what they believed. Long titles were popping out at me: "CIA Brainwashing Claim Is Rejected by Jury: Ex-Marine Convicted on Murder Charge", Ex-Marine blames slaying on insanity", Suspects 'fantasy' described", Killer guilty despite tale of brainwashing", CIA line disputed", and "Brainwashed" man convicted of murder". All of my journalism professors at Marshall had taught me to keep my headlines short. It was like looking at the tabloid covers in the line at the grocery store. There was a 1984 AP wire in Guam the read: Timothy McWilliams, who claimed he was tormented by memories of CIA brainwashing, convicted of murder. There were articles with shorter titles and smaller stories in "Around the Region" sections of newspapers. There was a lot of coverage. Combining the many news articles, I wrote the following:

On November 2, 1984, an ex-Marine, who claimed he was tormented by memories of CIA brainwashing, was convicted by a jury of six men and six women of murdering Alan Antonek and the malicious wounding of Michael Carter and Donald Askew. This was Timothy Allen McWilliams' second trial. His first trial ended in a mistrial on March 17, 1984. The defense had argued that McWilliams suffered from paranoid schizophrenia and was insane at the time of the shooting. McWilliams told his attorneys that he had been brainwashed to make him forget secret documents he had seen as a Marine Corps Embassy Guard in Saudi Arabia and Tunisia in the 1970's. Tim's lawyer referred to him as 'Timmy ' throughout both trials.

August 1, 1980, should have been like any other day in the lives of Timothy McWilliams and his three victims. Tim told investigators that he had been drinking wine and smoking pot at his home (44 Jones Ave.) and decided to go to a local bar, Finnerty's in the Sunnyside section of Morgantown.

There was a live performance that night. A young woman, Sandra Rae Griffith, was singing and playing guitar. She was 21-years-old. Tim sat at the bar and watched her perform. He had two beers and some gin. The owner of the bar, Robert "Bob" Coffman saw Tim there. Bob Coffman was also the bartender that night and his wife, Pricilla, was working the door. Sandra noticed Tim too because there were only eight or nine people at the bar that night. Sandra testified that she sang directly to Tim because she was getting any real reaction from him. He would nod at her and smirk, but she couldn't tell if he was into the music. At some point, Sandra broke a guitar string and went outside to fix it, when she came back; Tim was gone. Tim had been there about an hour when Alan Antonek, Michael Carter and Donald Askew came in for a beer and some foosball. Alan delivered cigarettes to Finnerty's every week and was known to Bob Coffman. Alan had also met Sandra Rae Griffith a few days before the shooting. He knew she was going to perform that night and wanted to watch her. Michael and Donald tagged along and went immediately to the game room.

George Stanley was the sound man for Sandra, and he was a sometimes a manager at Finnerty's for Bob Coffman. George stated that he noticed Tim leaning against the bar. He made it a point to notice who was around and what they were doing. He stated to police that Tim was applauding Sandra's singing, and guitar playing. He also saw Alan, Michael, and Donald that night. They were all outside together when Sandra broke a guitar string. When they came back into the bar, Tim was gone. George was able to identify Tim from a photo lineup.

According to Michael Carter's statement on August 3rd, 1980, *I went in the bar, sat down and had a couple of drinks, played some foosball, we were getting ready to listen to this chick sing and play the guitar. After around twelve, Alan said, "Let's go to Touch of Country. We said, "OK." As we were walking out the door, I saw Alan talking to that guy (Tim). I thought they knew each other or something. When we got outside, Alan told me that the guy had threatened to stuff him in a trunk. Alan told Michael that Tim was an ex-army man. I can't remember if they were arguing. I didn't recognize the guy until he came up to us. Alan said that the guy was*

following us. Alan then went up Stewart Street. Don and I
were crossing the Stadium Bridge. Apparently, this guy was
walking pretty fast. He catches up with us and asks us where
our little buddy is, and I go, I don't know" and he says, Why
not?" and I said, I can talk to you about it, and he says, I just
want to talk to your buddy, and by this time, Alan came
running up and comes up to him (Tim) and says, "What is your
problem, Buddy and the guy goes, "This" and he goes Bang.

Michael Carter graduated from WVU in 1984 and was
working as a lab consultant for Construction Materials at the
time of the trial. Michael during his trial testimony indicated
that Timothy McWilliams was the man in the bar and on the
bridge that night. Michael also stated that he thought that they
would have been "*alright*" if Alan hadn't come running up to
us. *I never expected to see no damn gun.* Michael indicated
that Tim had been dressed in blue jeans with a jean jacket,
glasses, and a beard. *It was just seconds, he was real close to*
Al, sticks it into him and I kind of jumps back and he gets me
in the arm, and as soon as he shoots me I just start running
and yelling for help and everything and then I hear another
one, he got Don.

47

Carter stated that the guy had a baseball cap on and it was a dark color either blue, green or red. He thought the emblem on the ballcap was "Mac." He states that the gun didn't look small, but he only got a glimpse of it. The guy (Tim) was carrying it in the shoulder area. He didn't see the holster, just the gun. His glasses were described as dark rimmed and round or octagon shaped. He repeated that the guy definitely had a beard. He re-stated that Alan came out of the Stadium Hill and crossed on the Lair side. Alan seemed to know that there was going to be a problem but Michael stated that he didn't think there was going to be a fight or anything. However, he said that he did pick up a bottle for protection. Michael said he wouldn't have known how to use it. He just wanted to talk with the guy.

In the trial testimony of Michael Carter, he explained that he had grown up in Elkins, West Virginia and graduated from St. Francis High School in 1979. Like Tim, Michael was a student at WVU at the time of the shooting. He knew Alan Antonek, and they had hung out together regularly. They went camping together. The night had started out at Warner Theatre. He met Alan at Maxwell's. They met up with

48

Donald Askew at the Mountainlair (also known as Blue Tic).
Alan wanted to go to Finnerty's where he knew a girl that was
going to be singing and playing the guitar. Alan was familiar
with Finnerty's because he delivered cigarettes there as part of
his vending machine job. He was an acquaintance of the
owner, Bob Kauffman.

The three were there for about an hour listening to
Sandra Rae Griffith perform. They drank at the bar and
played foosball. The truth may fall somewhere in the middle,
but Carter's testimony varied from his first police report to the
grand jury testimony, to the two trials. However, all of his
sworn statements and testimony recognize some level of
contact between Alan and Tim. As they left the bar, the
owner's wife (Pricilla) stopped Carter and Askew and took
away their beer bottles (because they still contained some
beer). Alan didn't have a drink with him, and he cut in front of
the other two to leave. After the three were outside, Alan told
Carter and Askew that a guy inside the bar had just threatened
to stuff him in a trunk. Then Alan indicated that this "guy"
was following them. Michael picked up a broken bottle. Alan

went around another way, and they split up. Michael Carter thought they were just going to another bar, Touch of Country.

McWilliams approached Donald and Michael and asked, where their buddy was? Michael and Donald told Tim that Alan had gone home. Tim turned to leave, but then Alan approached from the other side of the Stadium Bridge. Tim walked toward Alan then stepped back and shot him in the chest. He then turned and shot Carter and Askew. Michael stated that Alan dropped into the fetal position and made a loud noise. Then he remembered two shots. One shot hit Michael traveling into his forearm and then into his chest and abdomen. Michael got up and ran, collapsing near the back of the Mountainlair at a loading dock. The other shot hit Donald.

Donald also gave a statement. He stated that he was with Mike Carter *and I think the other kid's name was Alan. I didn't know the other kid that well. I was sitting with Mike at the bar, watching this girl sing. Alan came over, and we decided to leave. We walked out the door, and Alan said to walk down the street. We started walking towards the bridge, and I said, "Where is Alan going?" and Mike said, "some guy is following, so we went across the bridge, I remember yelling, "Walk up to the plaza, Alan." And then this guy, he must have followed us, came walking up to us and said, "Where is your friend at?" we said, "I don't know, why?" All of a sudden, Alan walked up behind us, and McWilliams just started walking towards Alan. We walked up to him, and he just stepped back, took the gun out and shot all three of us. He didn't seem angry. He just asked where Alan was in a normal tone of voice. I don't know if they had an argument. I didn't see Alan in the bar.* Asked to describe Tim's clothes, Donald Askew could not and he stated that he only saw his face.

Donald testified at trial. Donald Askew (then living in Cape Cod) was remodeling houses. Donald graduated with a degree in philosophy in 1984 from Wheeling College. He had been in Morgantown on summer break when he was shot. He graduated with Mike from St. Francis High School in 1979. Don went to junior high with Alan. He was a handyman at the time of the trial. Playing foosball and pool in the game room, he was supposed to go with David (his brother) to the movies but decided to go out instead with Mike. He was supposed to pick up his mother from work at

10:30 pm. He looked at his watch in Finnerty's, and it was 11:30 pm. He ran to the car, but it was gone. He called his mom from the pay phone near Dairy Queen, and she was pissed. He wanted her to come and get him so he could have the car and she said, "No." Donald stated that Tim walked up behind them very quick. Don asked Mike, "*Where is Alan going?*" Alan waived his hand. Tim asked, *"Where is your little friend?"* Don said, "*I don't know.*" Mike said, "*Can we help you*?" Tim turned and walked away. Alan appeared. Don didn't want a fight because he had a bad shoulder and it would fall out of joint. Tim followed Alan on the bridge. Alan said, *"What seems to be the problem?"* Tim shot all three in the mid-body. Donald ran across the street and collapsed. He was in the hospital two weeks and had a six-hour surgery. Donald remembered Tim's face and his strawberry blonde hair.

Alan H. Antonek, 18 years of age, of 628 Jones Ave. in Morgantown, WV was pronounced dead at 1 am on August 1, 1980, less than an hour after leaving Finnerty's Bar. He was taken to West Virginia University Medical Center and died of a gunshot to the abdomen. Alan Antonek was alive when he arrived at the hospital but barely. His blood pressure was dropping; his eyes were reactive but dilated. He was conscious at the scene, but by the time he arrived at WVU, he was not conscious. His condition continued to worsen, and no airway could be made. Alan succumbed to his injuries.

Per the autopsy: There was a gunshot wound to the upper anterior abdomen, distant, penetrating lethal liver, aorta, and thoracic vertebral column, muscles of the left back, and into the tissues of the subcutaneous tissue of the left back. The path was from front to back, right to left, and slightly from below upwards. The missile was recovered; large caliber, lead with an aluminum jacket, hollow point, not deformed. There were contusions and laceration of the heart and contusion of the lower lobes of both lungs. Antonek died of a gunshot wound to the abdomen through the liver and the aorta. The manner of death was a homicide.

Much would be made at trial of whether or not Alan and Tim argued that night at Finnerty's Bar. They did know each other as much as they lived on the same street. According to Tim, Alan had mentioned a 1978 dog shooting incident and the fact that Tim's truck had been recently vandalized. Tim told doctors that he thought it was Alan who vandalized the truck (there is not proof of that). Tim also said that Alan had threatened to "*call in the troops*" and teased him about shooting the tail off of a dog a few years earlier. Tim told doctors that Alan nudged him and slapped his head on the Stadium Bridge that night. Michael Carter and Donald Askew disputed those accounts.

Alan also had a blood alcohol level of 0.11 which is over the legal limit for driving (Alan was not driving). The is the equivalent of five beers. Witnesses at Finnerty's heard single words such as trouble and trunk. However, no one will ever know what the two discussed or argued about on that night. No matter what words were exchanged between the two at Finnerty's Bar, there would be no valid reason for Tim to shoot Alan and his friends.

Michael Anthony Carter was also in bad shape. He arrived at WVU about 30 minutes after the shooting. At first sight, it appeared he had been shot multiple times. He was alert and conscious at the scene, but his injuries were life-threatening. He complained of pain in his abdomen. There was massive bleeding coming from the wound in his arm.

Michael had been shot through the arm, and the bullet exited and traveled into his chest and down to his abdomen. His vitals remained strong, and he endured a long surgery. It took an x-ray to reveal that the bullet was lodged in his abdomen. His arm was broken and had to be splinted. Carter was in the hospital for 25 days recovering from his wounds. Michael had been able to run from the shooting site back to the loading dock behind the Lair before he collapsed. I tried to find Michael Carter for seven months so that I could interview him for this book. I was unable to locate him.

Donald Askew arrived at WVU in shock with internal bleeding. His wound was to the right rear abdomen. He was alert, but his vitals were not great when he arrived. He was complaining of leg pain and numbness when he tried to move his legs (this may have been the source for the family telling me that one of the boys was paralyzed). He suffered a left pleural effusion. He was the third victim to be shot. Askew was able to run across the street before he collapsed. He had a six-hour surgery and was in the hospital for two weeks. It was estimated that he was shot from less than five feet away. Like Michael Carter, Donald Askew had a long road to recovery. I was able to speak with Don's brother while writing this book. Donald did not want to be interviewed. His brother indicated that Don was doing well.

Other witnesses from that night also gave statements. Linda Molisee (who was employed at University Hospital, Station 31) stated that *I was stopped at a stop light near the scene at about midnight. I was looking at Red Beards, but it was closed, so I thought I would go on down and around and see what was going on in town. The person that was with me and I, we heard gunshots, and he stated that somebody got shot and I said, "are you sure it's not a backfire and he said, no that was gunshots." When the light began to change, a light blue pick-up truck came right on through, and there was a brown luxury car with a bunch of guys in it, they slammed on their brakes, and I remember watching their antenna flip back and forth and I went on around and I looked at the driver real close to see if he was going to pull out in front of me or something and anyway I got a good look at him. He had real wild brown curly hair, maybe shoulder length and as I went by him, he spoke to me. He said, "Hi." Both of our windows were down. I went on around, and as I came around there was a bunch of cars stopped, and the guy I was with said, "There is somebody up there lying in the road, are you going to go up" and I said, "Yes, I'll take my car and get it out of the way. I went on up, and there were maybe 15 people up by the top of the road looking down, and I saw a guy laying on the sidewalk screaming. When I got to him, there was another man there. A tall, stocky built fellow, he gave me a handkerchief. I put it on the guy's back, and he went and got me a rug to try and stop the guy's bleeding. Someone came across the street and said, "This other guy's hurt worse. I went across the street to work on him. The medical student was giving him CPR, and he preceded to vomit, and he ceased to breath, and we got his heart started again, and by then the EMS came. When asked about the sequence of the gunshots, Linda said, "There were three shots right in a row.*

Prosecutors asked if the any of the victims said anything. Linda stated that Donald Askew said, *"Oh my God. I've been shot. God Damn it hurts! Don't do that!"* Linda was applying pressure to his wound. Linda asked him if he knew who shot him and Donald said, *"No."*

Linda was asked if she saw anything on the Stadium Bridge that night. She stated that she saw someone walking toward the Sunny Side end. He was close to the end by the telephone booth. He was against the wall and walking normally. The implication was that she caught a glimpse of Tim as he crossed the bridge into Sunny Side. Prosecutors made the point that the person was walking normally, not walking fast, and was not running.

It would be revealed during the trial that police suspected Timothy Allen McWilliams almost right away. Based on the description of the shooter and his prior interactions with police, Tim quickly moved to the top of the suspect list. His strange behavior and the shooting of the dog two years prior made him a strong possibility as the perpetrator. Tim's photo was put in a photo line-up for witnesses, and his home was placed under surveillance. The work of solving the case began.

8 EVIDENCE

Based on medical evidence and eye-witness
testimony, a search warrant was drawn-up by investigators on
August 3, 1980. Items on the list were: .45 caliber pistol and
.45 caliber ammunition, a shoulder holster, any ball player
type hat or cap, blue jean pants, tee shirts (colored), blue jean
jacket, and eyeglasses, any military service records. The
address was 44 Jones Avenue occupied by one, Timothy Allen
McWilliams. It was a two-story brick house with a red &
white awning over the porch. Tim lived in the downstairs
bedroom. The home was located in Morgantown, Monongalia
County, West Virginia. Tim had already been identified by
one of the witnesses to the slaying. The bullet taken from the
body of Alan Antonek was a .45 caliber Winchester/Western

Super X Silver Tip hollow point. Officers had documentation that Timothy A. McWilliams had purchased the same type ammunition and pistol from Marstiller's Gun Shop in Morgantown one month prior to the day.

The warrant was served at 5:30 pm on August 3, 1980, shortly after Tim was arrested outside his apartment. The property receipt contained the following: 1 Detonics .45 caliber automatic pistol and clip, black leather Detonics gun case, High Standard Sport King .22 caliber pistol and clip, yellow and blue WVU ball cap, yellow and blue Mountaineer's Ball cap with Mountaineer emblem on the front, U.S. Marine Corps records of Timothy A. McWilliams, black clear frame glasses, black frame glasses, 3 pair of blue jeans, 1 pair of light corduroy pants, and a dark green corduroy jacket. Photos were taken of the .12 gauge shotgun Tim had used to shoot a dog in 1978. There is also no indication that any tee shirts were confiscated by the police during their search although they did take some pictures of a red shirt on the floor of the bedroom.

9 TRIALS AND TRIBULATIONS

By the time Tim's trial had moved through the judicial process and was ready to begin, the judge had ruled (1982), that McWilliams was not competent to stand trial and those rulings were extended in six-month intervals from 1982 until January of 1984. Tim had spent the better part of 18 months in the Monongalia County jail. The first prosecution doctors, Dr. Wilbur Sine (a psychiatrist) and Dr. Jo Ledwell (a psychologist) who interviewed Timothy McWilliams stated that he was competent to stand trial. However, some deficiencies appeared in the testing procedures used by Dr. Ledwell. Following that disclosure, the prosecution and the defense hired Dr. Patricia Williams and Dr. Joel Allen (respectively) to examine McWilliams, and both agreed that he was not competent to stand trial. He was sent to Weston State Hospital in hopes that his condition would improve.

The prosecutor, Thomas Newbraugh, and his assistant prosecutor (Bob Stone) had also sought to dismiss the case at one point by filing a motion of nolle prosequil (a dismissal) on July 16, 1982, but, Judge Frank DuPond overruled him. This fact would later become an appellate issue for the West Virginia Supreme Court in 1986. In March of 1984, McWilliams' first trial began. That trial ended in a hung jury three days later. Tim didn't speak to anyone (including his lawyers) during the first trial. McWilliams was then tried a second time. A second jury would decide his fate.

Timothy McWilliams told doctors that he had been injected with chemicals to erase his memory. As a member of the U.S. Marine Corps Embassy Guard and security guard at the embassy in Tunisia, McWilliams had top-secret security clearance as of 1973. He felt the government tried to erase the confidential data from his mind. Timothy's defense attorney (James Lees Junior) was quoted as saying, "*Tim's delusional state had him built into a fuse already.*" Tim explained to doctors that the government had forced him to participate in unnatural sex acts with orangutans so that they could later blackmail him over top-secret documents that he knew about. He also said that he had been decapitated by the CIA and that they had sewn his head back on afterward. McWilliams believed that agents periodically checked on him to make sure his memory had not returned. Timothy McWilliams was diagnosed by both prosecution and defense doctors as suffering from some form of schizophrenia. The issue was whether or not Tim was insane at the time of the shooting on August 1, 1980.

The six-man and six-woman jury that convicted Timothy McWilliams on Saturday, November 3, 1984, recommended mercy. The judge had no choice but to sentence Tim to 30 years. It was 10 years per count and they had to be served consecutively. While most news reports stated that McWilliams didn't know the three men that he shot, one paper reported that McWilliams and Antonek were neighbors living on the same street. The report stated that Antonek had teased McWilliams about shooting the tail off of a dog on July 11, 1978. The dog had been hiding in a bush near McWilliams apartment. The report also mentioned that Atonek had said something to McWilliams about his (McWilliams') truck being recently vandalized. There was no evidence that McWilliams knew Carter or Askew.

According to the prosecution's case, the military had not given Tim or anyone else a drug to make them forgot. The military stated that such a drug didn't exist. The military also denied these events (that McWilliams had described) at the embassy had ever happened. The prosecution (at first) had believed that Tim had made up all of the mental illness aspects of the case to explain away his shooting these three men after a bar fight. Eventually, though, the prosecution also came to believe that Tim was mentally ill (as he had been diagnosed) by doctors from both the defense and the prosecution. After the conviction, the appeals process began. The case would eventually be overturned by the West Virginia Supreme Court in 1986.

From 1980-1988, Tim would reside at either the Monongalia County Jail (which no longer exists) or Weston State Hospital (which closed in 1994) depending on the crowding situation at the hospital. After the reversal and acquittal, the WV Supreme Court gave the prosecutors 40 days to get Tim committed on civil order. If they could not accomplish this, Tim would have to be released into the public. He was committed to Weston on the Forensics Wing and then eventually to the last open wing of the hospital before its closure in 1994. Tim was released in 1988 to his parents.

The Opinion in McWilliams vs. West Virginia

December 19, 1986 (William T. Brotherton Jr.)

Courtesy West Virginia Supreme Court

BROTHERTON, Justice:

The appellant, Timothy McWilliams, appeals a Monongalia County Circuit Court jury verdict finding him guilty of first-degree murder with a recommendation of mercy, and guilty of two counts of malicious assault. The charges stemmed from an incident in which the appellant shot three young men, killing one and wounding the other two. The appellant's sole defense was insanity.

The appellant assigns the following errors: first, that the trial court improperly refused to grant the State's motion for an order of nolle prosequi; second, that the trial court improperly permitted the introduction of statements made by the appellant during a court-ordered psychiatric examination; third, that the trial court improperly instructed the jury on the disposition of the appellant if he was found not guilty by reason of insanity; fourth, that the trial court improperly quashed the subpoena of Prosecutor Thomas Newbraugh; fifth, that the trial court improperly excluded evidence of the appellant's mental condition subsequent to the shooting, and sixth, that the State failed to meet its burden of proving that the appellant was sane at the time of the shooting. We find merit in the final assignment of error, and reverse for failure to prove the appellant's sanity beyond a reasonable doubt.

On Friday evening, August 1, 1980, Timothy McWilliams entered Finnerty's, a nightclub located in the Sunnyside section of Morgantown. The victims, Allen Antonek, Michael Carter, and Donald Askew, entered the club sometime thereafter. During the course of the evening, bartender Robert Coffman overheard a portion of a conversation between McWilliams and Antonek while the two men were seated at the bar. One party stated something to the effect of: "If you want some trouble, I have got it for you," and the other party replied: "I have all the trouble you want."

*The three victims left Finnerty's sometime afterward. Upon exiting the club, Antonek told Carter that someone in the bar had threatened to stuff Antonek in a trunk. The victims walked toward the stadium bridge. McWilliams left the club a few minutes later. Antonek stated to his companions that someone was following them. He left the other two and took a circuitous route to the other side of the bridge. Carter and Askew proceeded across the bridge and were confronted at the other side by McWilliams. McWilliams asked them where their "little buddy" was, and Carter responded that he had gone home. McWilliams turned to leave, but at that moment Antonek appeared and asked what the problem was. McWilliams drew a .45 caliber pistol and shot Antonek. He then turned and shot Carter and Askew as they ran away. Antonek died from his wound. Carter and Askew recovered. The appellant's actions on the night of the crime appear in stark contrast to a very promising high school and early adult career. *124 Timothy McWilliams graduated from Buckhannon Upshur High School in 1971. He was a member of several athletic teams and was co-captain of the football team his senior year. His fellow students chose him to be a* *member of the homecoming court. He graduated in the top 10% of his class and scored in the 97th percentile on the American College Test (ACT).*

Following graduation, McWilliams enlisted in the United States Marine Corps. He was assigned to the prestigious embassy guard, and he served at the American Embassies in Saudi Arabia and Tunisia. The United States government granted him top secret clearance. He was honorably discharged in November 1975.

In January 1976, McWilliams enrolled as a full-time engineering student at West Virginia University. He initially performed quite well, but his grades deteriorated beginning in the summer of 1978. He failed or withdrew from most courses. His behavior also started to decline. McWilliams displayed many paranoid beliefs. He slept in his bathtub because he believed it would protect him if government agents tried to shoot him. He kept a shotgun in his apartment with shells lying in various places. He installed floodlights to illuminate his yard. He ate unusual foods in the belief that it would help his brain "regenerate." On July 11, 1978, he fired his shotgun into a bush, shooting the tail off a dog, in the belief that someone was in the bush who meant to do him harm.

McWilliams' pattern of unusual behavior continued thereafter through the night of the shootings on August 1, 1980.

McWilliams was arrested near his Morgantown apartment on August 3, 1980. On September 4, 1980, a Monongalia County grand jury indicted him for first-degree murder, W.Va.Code § 61-2-1 (1984), and two counts of malicious assault, W.Va.Code § 61-2-9 (1984).

Dr. Wilbur Sine, a psychiatrist, and Dr. Jo Ledwell, a psychologist, examined McWilliams following his indictment. By their reports, the trial court found McWilliams competent to stand trial by report dated June 11, 1981. However, certain deficiencies appeared in the testing procedures used by Dr. Ledwell. The trial court, therefore, ordered Dr. Patricia Williams, a psychiatrist, to perform further tests. Dr. Joel Allen, a psychiatrist retained by the defense, also examined McWilliams. The trial court held an evidentiary hearing on April 26, 1982, and concluded that McWilliams was not competent to stand trial. The trial court committed McWilliams to Weston State Hospital for a six-month improvement period under W.Va.Code § 27-6A-2 (1980). On

July 16, 1982, while McWilliams was at Weston, the State moved for an order of nolle prosequi. The trial court denied the motion. On November 10, 1982, the appellant requested continued treatment at Weston by motion under W.Va.Code § 27-6A-5 (1980). The trial court granted the motion. On April 21, 1983, the trial court ordered an additional improvement period for the appellant at Weston pursuant to W.Va.Code § 27-6A-2 (1980).

After McWilliams had undergone almost two years of treatment at Weston, the trial court held another evidentiary hearing and concluded that he was competent to stand trial. A jury trial began in Monongalia County Circuit Court on March 13, 1984. A mistrial was declared on March 17, 1984, after the jury was unable to reach a verdict. A second trial began on October 29, 1984. The jury returned the guilty verdicts on November 2, 1984.

I.

The appellant's first assignment of error is that the trial court improperly refused to grant the State's motion for an order of nolle prosequi. In support of its motion, the State noted that, at that time, three psychiatrists had examined McWilliams and that all three had concluded that McWilliams' mental disorder

interfered with his capacity to appreciate the criminality of his

acts.

The appellant argues that because of the volume of evidence

that McWilliams *125 was suffering from a mental disorder

which interfered with his criminal capacity, the trial court was

required to grant the State's motion. We do not agree. A

prosecutor cannot dismiss criminal charges without the prior

approval of the court. See syl. pt. 1, Denham v. Robinson, 72

W.Va. 243, 77 S.E. 970 (1913); W.Va.R. Crim.P. 48(a). The

State sought approval from the trial court for dismissing the

charges, but was denied. If the trial court was required to

grant the motion, the requirement that court approval be

obtained to dismiss criminal charges would be rendered

meaningless.

In support of his argument, the appellant cites syllabus point 1

of State ex rel. Walton v. Casey, 163 W.Va. 208, 258 S.E.2d

114 (1979), which states: "A criminal trial is unwarranted

when pretrial psychiatric examinations clearly reveal by a

preponderance of the evidence, that the accused at the time

the crime was committed, was not criminally responsible for his acts." However, we have stated that the decision whether to adopt the policy of this rule is within the discretion of the trial court and the prosecutor. State ex rel. Smith v. Scott, ___ W.Va. ___, 280 S.E.2d 811, 814 (1981). Absent an abuse of discretion, we will not disturb a decision made by the trial court and the prosecutor on this issue. On the facts of this case, we find no abuse of discretion. Therefore, we find no error in the denial of the State's motion.

II.

The appellant's second assignment of error is that the trial court improperly permitted the introduction of statements made by the appellant during a court-ordered psychiatric examination. Dr. Patricia Williams performed the examination as ordered by the trial court over the appellant's objection after the State moved for additional psychiatric evaluation. The appellant called Dr. Williams to testify at trial during the appellant's case-in-chief. On cross-examination, the State elicited from Dr. Williams several statements McWilliams made during the examination concerning his ability to understand the criminality of his actions.[1] The appellant argues that the admission of those statements

violated his constitutional privilege against self-incrimination.

During his direct examination, the appellant's counsel asked

Dr. Williams whether McWilliams knew that Antonek was not

a government agent, and Dr. Williams responded that

McWilliams stated that he "knew he [Antonek] was not the

CIA."[2] Because the appellant's sole defense was insanity,

Dr. Williams' testimony was potentially incriminating because

it concerned criminal responsibility.[3] During its cross-

examination, the State asked the following questions:

Q. And after shooting the boys, he told you he knew it was a

crime, didn't he? A. That's correct. Q. He just came out and

said: I knew it was a crime, and he ran to avoid detection? A.

Actually he said he was gonna go back to his apartment and

think about it for a while. That was his exact statement. Q.

And also, when he says he knew that the police were looking,

or were in the neighborhood, were watching him, then he went

to get a bus ticket to leave town? A. That is correct. *126 Q.

Mr. Stone just pointed out to me in your report that he said to

you, I think his exact words were that after the shooting he

states he knew it was a crime and therefore he wanted to get away so that he would not be arrested? A. (The witness nods in the affirmative.)

In State v. Jackson, ___ W.Va. ___, 298 S.E.2d 866 (1982), we examined a situation where, under court order, the defendant was examined by a court-appointed psychiatrist to determine his competency to stand trial. We held that the psychiatrist's testimony should not contain any incriminating statements made by the defendant. However, under the facts of that case, it was the prosecution who was offering the psychiatrist as a witness and not the defense. In this case, the defendant put the psychiatrist on the stand and explored in depth the doctor's examination of Mr. McWilliams. The State's cross-examination touched the same subject matter as the defendant's direct examination and was not objected to at the time. The defendant should not now be able to complain about the cross-examination when it was the defendant's questions on direct which opened and thoroughly explored the subject matter of the cross-examination.

The standard which controls the admissibility of this testimony is found in syllabus point 2 of State v. Bowman, 155 W.Va. 562, 184 S.E.2d 314 (1971): "An appellant or plaintiff in error will not be permitted to complain of error in the admission of evidence which he offered or elicited, and this is true even of a defendant in a criminal case." Because the appellant's counsel opened the door to the State's cross-examination by questioning Dr. Williams about the statements McWilliams made during the psychiatric examination, the appellant may not complain of error in the State's exploration on cross-examination of other statements made during the same psychiatric examination touching the same subjects as brought up by the defense.

III.

The appellant's third assignment of error is that the trial court improperly instructed the jury on the disposition of the appellant if he was found not guilty by reason of insanity. The trial court gave an instruction which completely covered the procedure for hospitalization of defendants found not guilty by reason of insanity.[4] The appellant regarded the instruction as highly prejudicial and initially requested that the jury be instructed not to consider post-trial disposition.[5] When the trial court refused to give such an instruction, the appellant offered a different disposition instruction which he requested be given in lieu of the trial court's instruction.[6] The trial court refused on the ground that the offered instruction was not complete.

"In any case where the defendant relies upon the defense of insanity, the defendant is entitled to any instruction which advises the jury about the further disposition of the defendant in the event of a finding of not guilty by reason of insanity which correctly *127 states the law." Part syl. pt. 2, State v. Nuckolls, ___ W.Va. ___, 273 S.E.2d 87 (1980). Nuckolls expressly overruled the prior rule that an instruction on the disposition of a defendant after a verdict of not guilty by reason of insanity is not proper. See syl. pt. 6, State v. Grimm, 156 W.Va. 615, 195 S.E.2d 637(1973).[7]

The law controlling the disposition of a defendant who is found not guilty by reason of insanity is found in W.Va.Code § 27-6A-3 (1980). "An instruction which attempts to explain under what circumstances a criminal defendant who has been involuntarily committed to a mental institution subsequent to a verdict of not guilty by reason of insanity may be discharged from the mental institution must include an adequate and accurate explanation of the law relating to commitment and

discharge of involuntary patients at state mental institutions."
Syl. pt. 6, State v. Boyd, ___ W.Va. ___, 280 S.E.2d 669
(1981) (emphasis added). Boyd requires that any instruction
on the disposition of a defendant after a verdict of not guilty
by reason of insanity include a complete explanation of the
procedure for involuntary commitment and discharge as given
in the Code.

The appellant's original proposed instruction on disposition
did not correctly state the law as required by Nuckolls; it did
not state any law. The appellant's second proposed instruction
on disposition did not provide a complete explanation of all
phases of the civil commitment process as required by Boyd.
The trial court's instruction did explain the process
completely. The appellant raised no specific objection to the
trial court's instruction, but rather insisted upon amending his
own instruction in order to make it acceptable to the trial
court. A defendant is not entitled to amend his own instruction
in order to bring the instruction into compliance with the law
when the trial court's instruction on the issue accurately and
adequately covers the procedure and when the defendant
makes no specific objection to the trial court's instruction. We

therefore find no error in the instruction given by the trial court on the disposition of a defendant after a verdict of not guilty by reason of insanity

IV.

The appellant's fourth assignment of error is that the trial court improperly quashed the subpoena of Prosecutor Thomas Newbraugh. The appellant subpoenaed Newbraugh for trial for the purpose of testifying to a statement which he made in a motion for an order of nolle prosequi in this case. The motion states as follows:

That, if the above-captioned matters were to proceed to trial, the State would be without any evidence to rebut [sic] an insanity defense.

The appellant argues that the statement should have been treated as a judicial admission which is conclusive as to its content. We do not agree. A judicial admission is a concession made by a party for the purpose of withdrawing a particular fact from the realm of dispute. See, e.g., Outer Banks Contractors, Inc. v. Forbes, 302 N.C. 599, 604, 276 S.E.2d 375, 379 (1981). In order to constitute a judicial admission, the statement must be one of fact, not opinion. See, e.g., Hedge

v. Bryan, 425 S.W.2d 866, 868 (Tex.Civ.App.1968).

The statement in question here is opinion. The State made the

statement in support of a motion, not as an admission of fact.

A statement made by an attorney which amounts to an opinion

on the strength or weakness of a case is not relevant and is not

admissible as evidence. See DiBella v. County of Suffolk, 574

F. Supp. 151, 154 (E.D.N.Y.1983), aff'd., 762 F.2d 990 (2d

Cir.1983). We therefore find no error in the trial court's

decision to quash the subpoena of the prosecutor.

*128 V.

The appellant's fifth assignment of error is that the trial court

improperly excluded evidence of the appellant's mental

condition subsequent to the shootings. During direct

examination, the appellant asked Dr. Patricia Williams about

her opinion as to McWilliams' competency to stand trial after

she examined him in 1982. The State objected on the ground

that a defendant's competency to stand trial is not relevant to

the jury. The trial court sustained the objection. The appellant

now argues that the question was an attempt to elicit

circumstantial evidence relating to McWilliams' mental condition at the time of the shootings.

The determination of the accused's competency to stand trial is solely for the judge and is of no concern to the jury. State ex rel. Smith v. Scott, ___ W.Va. ___, 280 S.E.2d 811, 814 (1981). The question the appellant asked of Dr. Williams was improper as it was phrased. However, the confusion was compounded by the trial court's ruling that the appellant would only be permitted to "elicit testimony that goes to his [McWilliams'] mental status at the time of the shooting." While the ultimate issue is the accused's mental condition at the time of the offense, evidence of the accused's mental condition either before or after the offense is admissible so far as it is relevant to the accused's mental condition at the time of the offense. Id., 280 S.E.2d at 813.

We agree with the appellant that McWilliams' mental condition at the time of Dr. Williams' examination in 1982 is relevant on the issue of criminal responsibility. Expert psychiatric opinions on the issue of criminal responsibility will never be based upon examinations which took place at the time the offense was committed. Psychiatrists will not be present and available to conduct examinations at the scene of the crime. A psychiatrist can do no better than to determine the accused's mental condition at the time of the examination, which may be either before or after the time of the offense, and then to give an opinion as to whether the accused's mental condition at the time of the offense was the same or different. However, we believe that the trial court's ruling on the question as it was phrased at trial was proper.

VI.

The appellant's primary assignment of error is that the State failed to meet its burden of proving that the appellant was sane at the time of the shootings. We agree, and we therefore reverse.

"There exists in the trial of an accused a presumption of sanity. However, should the accused offer evidence that he was insane, the presumption of sanity disappears and the burden of proof is on the prosecution to prove beyond a reasonable doubt that the defendant was sane at the time of the offense." Syl. pt. 2, State v. Milam, 163 W.Va. 752, 260 S.E.2d 295 (1979). In this case, the appellant presented evidence of insanity through Dr. Patricia Williams, a

psychiatrist who had examined McWilliams in 1982. Dr. Williams discussed her examination of McWilliams and testified that she had diagnosed him as a paranoid schizophrenic. She described McWilliams' many delusions and the effect they had on his ability to cope with the world. Dr. Williams stated that within a degree of medical certainty, McWilliams was not sane at the time of the shootings. On cross-examination, the State elicited testimony from Dr. Williams that McWilliams had stated to her that he knew he had committed a crime.[8] However, Dr. Williams maintained that McWilliams was not sane. She noted that individuals who are not criminally responsible often insist that they knew what they were doing, while the reverse is often true for individuals who are criminally responsible.[9] The appellant also presented several lay witnesses *129 who knew McWilliams before the shootings. They testified that he had been a normal high school student but that his behavior had become unusual after his discharge from the Marines.

The State presented no expert testimony to support McWilliams' sanity, and relied entirely upon lay testimony by witnesses who did not know McWilliams before the night of the shootings.[10] The State did present some slight evidence that McWilliams had argued with Antonek inside the club and that the argument could have provoked the attack.[11]

The State had the burden to rebut the appellant's substantial evidence of insanity and to prove that McWilliams was sane at the time of the shootings beyond a reasonable doubt. The State did not meet its burden. The evidence presented in this case is similar to evidence presented in Milam, where we also reversed because the State failed to meet its burden of proof.

In Milam, the State presented no lay or expert testimony to rebut the expert psychiatric testimony of insanity presented by the defendant. The defendant demonstrated that the psychiatric disability existed before the time of the offense. Id., 163 W.Va. at 764, 260 S.E.2d at 302. We concluded that the State had not presented any proof of the defendant's sanity, and that double jeopardy principles barred retrial. Id., 163 W.Va. at 765-66, 260 S.E.2d at 302-03.

We noted in Milam, and we continue to believe, that "it is not possible to fashion a particular rule on whether the State has failed to carry its burden of proving sanity beyond a reasonable doubt." Id., 163 W.Va. at 764, 260 S.E.2d at 302.

*Each case will differ in the amount and type of evidence
needed to meet the burden of proving sanity. In this case, the
State presented only lay witnesses. Even though we conclude
that their testimony was insufficient to prove sanity, we do not
mean to say that lay testimony can never rebut expert
testimony. "The testimony of expert witnesses on an issue is
not exclusive, and does not necessarily destroy the force or
credibility of other testimony." Part syl. pt. 2, Webb v.
Chesapeake and Ohio Ry., 105 W.Va. 555, 144 S.E. 100
(1928), cert. denied, 278 U.S. 646, 49 S. Ct. 82, 73 L. Ed. 559
(1928).*

*Lay witnesses may give an opinion about the mental condition
of a criminal defendant. "When the question of mental
capacity of one charged with a crime to commit it is involved,
a non-expert witness may be allowed to express his opinion,
where he has personal knowledge of the facts on which his
opinion is based." Syl. pt. 4, State v. Fugate, 103 W.Va. 653,
138 S.E. 318 (1927). See also W.Va.R.Evid. 701. In addition,
lay witnesses may testify as to facts concerning the criminal
defendant's behavior, thereby providing the jury with the*
information needed to *reach a conclusion about the*

defendant's mental condition. When lay witnesses testify about a person's mental condition, the following factors are to be considered: (1) the witnesses' acquaintance with the person and opportunity to observe the person's behavior;[12] (2) the time during which the observation occurred;[13] and (3) the nature of the behavior observed.[14]

*130 In this case, none of the State's witnesses knew Timothy McWilliams before the night of the shootings. The State did not produce any witnesses, such as McWilliams' neighbors or professors, who knew him before the shootings and who could testify about his behavior. None of the State's witnesses had had a sufficient opportunity to observe McWilliams to enable them to testify about his mental condition. The State produced no evidence of any reason, other than a slight provocation, why McWilliams shot and killed a young man he barely knew, and shot and wounded two young men he did not know at all. "[T]he State's burden of proving sanity beyond a reasonable doubt does not mean that the sanity evidence must be entirely without contradictions." State v. Kinney, ___ W.Va. ___, 286 S.E.2d 398, 401 (1982). However, the case before us is not one in which a factual contradiction on the issue of sanity

appears. The facts presented point conclusively to McWilliams' insanity at the time of the offense.

As a result of our decision in this case, McWilliams will be acquitted. The State will have the opportunity to initiate involuntary civil commitment proceedings against him. In those proceedings, the State will have the burden of proving by clear, cogent, and convincing evidence that McWilliams is presently mentally ill and that because of his illness he is likely to cause serious harm to himself or others if he is allowed to remain at liberty.[15] If the State fails to meet its burden, McWilliams will be a free man. We are troubled by this prospect, but no alternative exists under West Virginia law.

Under the Milam rule there exists at trial a presumption of sanity unless the accused should offer evidence of insanity, in which case the State has the burden at trial to prove a defendant sane beyond a reasonable doubt, just as it must prove every other element of an offense. If the State fails to meet its burden and the defendant is found not guilty by reason of insanity, the State then has the burden during the involuntary civil commitment hearing to prove that the defendant is mentally ill by clear, cogent, and convincing evidence. The difference in the burdens of proof creates a gap through which a defendant may pass. The State may not be able to prove either that the defendant was sane at the time of the offense beyond a reasonable doubt or that he is mentally ill at the time of the involuntary civil commitment hearing by clear, cogent, and convincing evidence. As a result, a defendant who has committed a crime may neither serve time in the penitentiary nor undergo treatment at a mental institution. It would appear that some legislation is needed to fill this gap. We note that several other jurisdictions have developed methods for dealing with this problem.[16]

*131 For the above reasons, we reverse the jury verdict of the Circuit Court of Monongalia County and order that a judgment of acquittal be entered. This order shall be stayed for forty days to give the State the opportunity to initiate involuntary mental commitment procedures pursuant to W.Va. Code §§ 27-6A-3 and 27-5-4 (1980).

Reversed and remanded with directions.

The court instructs the jury that in the event the defendant is found not guilty by reason of insanity that this court may order that he be hospitalized in a mental health facility for observation and examination. You are further instructed that during such observation period procedures for civil commitment may be initiated before the court by the prosecuting attorney or any other interested party; however, in the event the defendant is not found to be insane at the time, the defendant may be released.

10 LEO

Norman Leonard McWilliams or "Leo" or "Mac" was one of my favorite members of the family. He was born in 1933 but was young at heart. He was friendly to me, and he was nice to me until the end. I tried to call him Mr. McWilliams (in the beginning), but he insisted that I call him "Leo." He made me feel like part of the family from the start. He taught me things about animals and gardening. He told me once that there was no point in shooting an opossum in the head. Leo said that they were double or triple skulled and it would not kill them. It had to be a body shot. He said that he had once shot an opossum in the head and then buried it. The same night he heard a bunch of commotion in the dog pen. The opossum was alive and well and attacking his dogs.

89

He taught me how to play spades. He had a huge personality and smile. Leo listened to old country music and was a fixture at the kitchen table in the evenings. One could tell that he worked hard. His hands were calloused and stained with unforgiving grease. Leo often looked tired. He had bags under his eyes. He taught machine shop to high school students. He had land to take care of and animals to feed. There was the feral black cat that he had tamed enough that it would come in the house to eat and lie behind him while he sat at the kitchen table but only Leo could pet it. He would pour it a dish of milk and the cat would purr.

Leo had two Old English Bulldogs (Mr. T and Cora Lee). They were brother and sister. They were family pets and much loved. Leo wanted to start a kennel and do some breeding. He would lend out Mr. T to stud for either a fee or pick of the litter (whatever was in the contract). He would breed Cora Lee. She became pregnant once while I was dating Jeff. I think there were about six puppies. We stayed at their house and helped take care of them. The puppies couldn't be left with the mother alone because she was huge and could accidentally roll over on them. They might suffocate. It was a process. They needed to feed every two hours. A warm wet cloth would be put on their little butts to get them to pee and poop every couple of hours. They were adorable, but it was hard work. Leo taught me a lot about breeding and taking care of puppies. We were both animal lovers.

I watched horrified one day when Cora Lee passed out in the front yard. Her eyes rolled to the back of her head. I thought she was dead. Leo pumped her chest and breathed into her mouth until she came back to life. Leo taught me about putting lemon juice in the dog's throat if it got choked and couldn't breathe. Leo showed me some things about gardening and once told me not to cut the grass in my bikini because it was causing a traffic jam. He had a good sense of humor. Leo introduced me to the Red Eye (tomato juice and beer) not my favorite. He was just a good man. He always made feel at home. He wore work pants and button-down shirts with short sleeves. His white undershirt was always showing around his neck. His smile was contagious, and he loved to laugh.

Leo was from an extremely rural area of West Virginia (Grafton). He once told me that when he was a little boy, he had never seen a black person. One day, there was a knock at the door, and Leo answered it. A black man stood before him, and Leo started screaming and running down the hall. Leo said it nearly scared him to death. He said his parents sat him down and gave him a stern talking to because they were afraid that Leo's reaction had embarrassed the poor man. Leo told me that he still felt terrible about that incident.

Leo worked hard, and he had expectations that others would work hard too. Former students came to visit him. People who worked with him remembered him fondly. His children worked hard after his example. People remembered him in the condolences section of his obituary as being a great teacher and father. Former students left him comments. He was respected and honored by many who knew him. I knew when Jeff and I broke up that I would miss Leo the most. He was a really good person.

Leo's Obituary from The Record Delta a few days after his
death:

Norman "Leo" (MAC) McWilliams, 84, of Buckhannon,
passed on March 8, 2018, after a lengthy battle with dementia
and Alzheimer's. Leo was born in Grafton, WV on September
28, 1933, the youngest of eight (8) children born to the late
Dorsey Robert and Bessie Lucinda (Smith) McWilliams all of
whom preceded him in death. He was united in marriage on
April 11, 1952, to Virginia Ann (Bosley) McWilliams who
survives. He is also survived by son Timothy McWilliams of
Buckhannon; daughter Rita Yaun and husband Ed, and
granddaughter Melinda Sanders and great granddaughter
▅▅▅ of Orlando, FL and granddaughter Haley Burton of
North Palm Beach, FL; son, Mark McWilliams and wife
Deanna, grandson Matthew of Palm City, FL; son, Jeff
McWilliams and wife Jennifer and granddaughter Jordan and

grandson ▮ *of Birmingham, AL. He is survived by two (2) adopted granddaughters: Missy Callahan and husband Adam Tipton and great-grandson* ▮ *of Greensboro, NC and* ▮ *Callahan Burns and husband Matt and great granddaughter* ▮ *and great-grandson* ▮ *of Summersville, WV. Leo was retired from teaching machine shop at the Fred Eberle Vocational School in Buckhannon. Leo loved life and was always smiling, laughing and enjoyed his family, friends, and neighbors. He had a passion for animals and was known throughout the Southeast for one of the premier kennels for Old English Bulldogs. The family would like to thank the many special neighbors and friends for prayers, food, phone calls, visits, and help running errands. Arrangements are being made through Poling-St. Clair Funeral Home and his body is being cremated for a family memorial service later this Summer. Online condolences may be made to the family at www.polingstclair.com. We know that in all things God works for the good of those who love him. Romans: 8:28.*

11 MEETING TIM

The first time I met Tim was quite nerve-wracking. I
went to Buckhannon with Jeff for the weekend. I was
nervous. I remember my stomach having that falling feeling
when we pulled into the driveway. The sound of the gravel
was pulsating in my ears. It was still light out but barely. The
outline of the house was against the sky. I could smell
Ginny's country cooking in the kitchen, from the car. I walked
in and there he was. I could only see his back. He was
wearing a plaid shirt, jeans, and a ball cap. Tim didn't turn
around. He wore large glasses. Leo was at the kitchen table
with Tim. Leo was shuffling cards. Ginny was hovering over
the stove. I could hear the laundry running and smelled dryer
sheets. All was normal except there was a killer sitting at the

kitchen table. Leo introduced us. Tim didn't try and shake my hand. He just looked up and said, "Hello Kim." in a monotone detached voice. He was a bit disheveled. He had about two days of five o'clock shadow. His hair was dark brown and messy. He looked like Jeff, just older. He was very quiet. Too quiet. Leo and Tim went on playing cards while Jeff and I got settled. I could hear my own heart beating.

We had a quiet dinner. The Ferrell cat was sitting behind Leo's head wagging its tail as if it knew something I didn't know. When Tim was done eating, he got up and shuffled away in slippers. He was bent over like an old man, and he shuffled when he walked. He seemed to be heavily medicated. Ginny grabbed his dish and took it the sink. She began washing the dishes. We all finished eating, and we cleared the table. Tim came back, and we all played cards for a while. I could not sleep. Once Tim went up to the attic bedroom, I was wide awake. Tim was rocking in the rocking chair up there. Squeak, squeak squeak. The rocking chair was squeaking back and forth and back and forth. Tim was mumbling. I was frozen with fear. I had never experienced anything like it.

He never touched me. We never shook hands. He would say, "Hello, Kim." and I would say, "Hello Tim." We would play hearts. We watched football. Sometimes, we sat on the deck. He chuckled a few times to himself and I found that unsettling. Ginny directed Tim to do this or that. She would tell him to say this or that. He always looked sickly and disheveled. He continued to shuffle and appear heavily medicated. I guess I thought or hoped Tim would get better. I thought he might act or look like that picture behind the couch on the wall, but he did not get better. Tim just existed.

Researching Tim, I can't find where he was ever counted in a census after 1980 at WVU. He has no work record since the military. His only address is the one with his parents. Tim has no listed cell phone. His number is listed as the same landline that his parents have had since I knew them. There is no evidence that Tim owned a car. He has no social media presence. He has never married or had children. He seemed to have stood in one place for thirty years.

12 SPOKANE

It was 2018 and I was visiting Spokane, Washington. I love, to go west. I could live in Seattle if not for the rain. I love the state of Washington, and so when I got a chance to visit Spokane, I jumped on it. We were there about five days. The weather was not as bad as Seattle. There was some sunshine. Spokane reminded me of a smaller Denver with a population of 250k instead of 2.5 million. I was on west coast time, so when my phone buzzed at 5am, I growled. My room had electric blinds, so I didn't even know if it was daylight. I looked at the time on the table clock and rolled my eyes to the back of my head. I am not a morning person. I am not even a mid-morning person. My friends know this fact, my east-coast friends sometimes forget, and I forgive them.

Brian sleepily handed me the phone. He went to fetch Starbucks before I turned into a monster of biblical proportions. It was Buddy. Buddy was one of my best friends from college. Buddy (Kenneth Davidson) was the person through whom I had met Jeff at Marshall. There are people who only text or call when something has happened. Normally, I just talked with Buddy over Facebook. I called Buddy, and he told me that Tim McWilliams had killed Leo. My mind was blown. I had not thought about that family in years. About five years ago, Rita Yaun (Rita McWilliams) had shown up on Facebook page under, "People You May Know." We had a mutual friend. I blocked her and then searched for other family members with the intention of blocking them as well. It wasn't that they had done something to me. I just didn't want an awkward situation. If I could see her then she could see me.

Buddy explained that Tim slit his father's throat at about 6 am the previous morning. Buddy's dad and Leo had worked together for years in the school system. They were close. Buddy explained that Tim had a knife wound too but that no one knew what had happened. Buddy wanted to know when

Tim had gotten out of the mental institution (Weston State Hospital). He was surprised to learn that Tim was home before Jeff and I had broken up. Buddy said that he never knew that Tim was out. Buddy and his dad thought that he was incarcerated at either a prison or mental hospital. Leo never told Buddy's dad that Tim was out and living at home. Buddy sent me the news link, and we wrapped up the conversation. I asked Buddy to send me the obituary if there was one. Brian was waiting when I disconnected, and I told him what had happened. He was shocked. I had told Brian the whole story years before. It was a gloomy revelation.

Over the next two days, there were about ten stories about the crime and the arrest. The narrative was much the same. This was an early morning crime where a Buckhannon man stabbed his father. Then the narrative began to change. Some news outlets were stating that Leo had Alzheimer's Disease and dementia. No news outlets were mentioning that Tim was a schizophrenic. No news outlets were mentioning that Tim had shot three people in 1980 and that one of those people had died. There was no mention of the fact that Tim had been living with his parents under the radar for almost 30 years. This was a famous West Virginia Supreme Court case that is still cited as precedent today. The questions that were not being asked were driving me crazy. All one had to do was google Tim's name, and the case popped right up. No one asked why a 65- year-old schizophrenic was living with his two 84- year-old parents (one of which was suffering from Alzheimer's and dementia). Three other siblings lived in Florida and Alabama.

All of this fogged my mind for a couple of days. It had been 30 years, but I felt so sorry for Leo. I read that Tim might be claiming self-defense and my mind was boggled. I had always thought that Tim might kill someone again, but I thought it would be in those first five years or so after being released from Weston State Hospital. Back in the late 80's, Tim didn't seem like he would fit back into regular society. I didn't think he would acclimate. He seemed like a zombie who had been thrown into a whole new world. I didn't know it would take 30 years.

I had a few nightmares in Spokane, and I didn't sleep well the rest of the trip. They were the same nightmares I used to have when I first found out about Tim. I was also a thousand miles away on the rest of the trip. I experienced the beauty and the waterfalls. They calmed me, but it was at a distance. I took a lot of photos. There was a coffee shop named, *Atticus.* I love it. I am a sucker for anything from, *To Kill A Mockingbird.* There was a game store, *Boo Radley's.* I spent a lot of time in a bookstore, *Auntie's.* Brian and I took walks and ate some tasty sushi, but I was living in two places in my head.

I experienced Spokane but from a distance. We crossed the border into Idaho and went to a lake in Coeur d' Alene. It was gorgeous, but I was distracted. Brian kept trying to pull me back into the present but, I was deeply bother by this situation. I ate dinner with these people. I played cards with them. I sat on the porch with Leo and Tim. I felt thrust back into that time. I never pondered on my relationship with Jeff. I made the right decision, and I moved on. I was an unpleasant time, and I do not like to re-visit it. I have married for 27 years, and I have a super family and wonderful children. I have been lucky. Now, I was being thrust back into my old apartment at Marshall. The carpet was brown shag, the walls were wood paneling, the couches were pink with white dots, and the drapes were orange. There was a creepy laundry room in the dungeon of a basement there. I started thinking about Puky, my college cat, who lived to be twenty-years-old.

Running through my mind was the campus at Marshall. I remembered the park by the Ohio River and the Huntington Bus Station. I remembered the walls and smells of the journalism school. It was always cold. I could picture the student center and the memorial. I could see the twin towers where I lived my freshman year. There was the MU Bookstore where they would sell you a book for fifty dollars and then offer you two dollars on the return. The was the Radisson where I worked with Brian up and until we moved to Denver in 1990.

My brain ran through the McWilliams' house. The colors, the furniture, and the smells came to me. I remembered the bulldogs and the black Ferrell cat. I could smell the grass and the garden. I could clearly see the attic bedroom. The room had a low ceiling and it was hard to imagine three boys living up there. The room was not large. The carpet and bedspread may have been red. Their births were far apart so, I suspect there were not three of them up there for long. Tim would have been about thirteen when Jeff was born. My guess is that the back room may have been built for Rita. There was a larger bedroom between the back bedroom and the living/tv room. Leo and Ginny slept there. There was a small area like a foyer where the stairs to the attic bedroom stood. The front door was there but no one used it. Everyone used the door to the kitchen and the kitchen was the largest room in the house. There was a lot of woodwork with beige, brown and tan colors. The master bedroom was blue. The memories were flooding back.

13 THE NEWS

It was in the first week in Spokane that I considered writing this book. A couple of days after the first article appeared in the local West Virginia newspapers, I noticed that the article about the murder was on the same page (on-line) as Leo's obituary. The murder case told the story of Leo McWilliams being stabbed in the neck by his son. Leo was already dead when EMTs arrived to treat the wound on Tim's forearm. The obituary of Leo McWilliams states that Leo died after a long battle with dementia and Alzheimer's. This disturbed me. I can understand not wanting to write in the obituary that Leo was stabbed in the neck by his son, I don't think (however) that people should be misled about the cause of the death. Leo didn't die of natural causes. I am not sure why the newspaper printed it.

I felt this was a disservice to Leo. The family had already told the press they were standing by Tim and that he may have killed his father in self-defense. What better way to lay the foundation than to push the narrative that Leo died after battling dementia and Alzheimer's Disease. It implies that his death was his fault. News stories reported that Tim climbed on his father's back and slit his throat while Leo was face down on the floor. All of this information bothered me as someone who had once been close to the family. For over two years, Leo was like a father to me. I thought he deserved better.

All of this brought me back to their kitchen table in Buckhannon in 1987 and 1988. Once I knew about Tim, all of the discussions around the table was how the family was going to get Tim home from Weston State Hospital. Jeff had told me that his parents took out additional loans and mortgages to pay for Tim's defense and legal bills. Ginny was working as a bus aide for the school district. Leo worked as a machine shop teacher. The family continuously strategized about ways to get Tim home. I often wondered if home was the best place for Tim.

I remember the family stating that Tim was the head of security in Tunis. I don't know if that is true. They also noted that Tim was Henry Kissinger's personal body guard when he was in Tunisia and I don't know if that is true. I remember that the family told me that Tim's defense attorney tried to subpoena Bob McNamara during the trials. I was not able to verify these statements in my research. The family blamed the military and government for Tim's condition. They were willing to go to great lengths to get Tim home. This subject dominated family discussion from the time I found out about the shootings.

14 WESTON STATE HOSPITAL

On May 26, 2018, I took a historical tour of Weston State Hospital. I would have to say that my sense of smell was the predominant force. Follow your nose. The building is so beautiful from the outside and it reminded me of the Biltmore in North Carolina. The architecture is stunning. The building is stoic. It is a façade, however, to cover the true ugliness and heartbreak I felt on the inside. Musty smells filled the lobby. Beautifully polished wood stood out against what could only be described as horrible living conditions for patients there. I wanted to get an idea of what Tim would have experienced from 1980-1988 while he was residing on and off at the facility. For a time after the West Virginia Supreme Court overturned his conviction, Tim would have resided on the last open ward before Weston closed in 1994.

Once one moved from the highly decorated lobby to the patient ward, the smell changes to one of mothballs, mice, and mold. The paint peeling from the yellow walls was possibly a vain attempt to escape as well. There were holes in the walls and the ceilings. While most of the hallways were painted yellow, patient room were white, baby blue, pink, mint green, and turquoise. Bent bedframes and faded fabric on chairs reminders of a different time.

The damp feeling was thick and unforgiving. The rust and brokenness provoke a sadness in me that made me wonder how it might feel to have a family member residing in a place like this. They would be trapped by loneliness and shadows of what once was a fancy hospital in another age and time. The peeling paint a reminder of how things were and would never be again. This was a perfect metaphor for many patients there, I am sure. The rooms were now empty and silent but need only close their eyes and imagine the sounds and smells of overcrowding. I could imagine screaming, loud talk and metal banging together in a very busy hospital. Nurses would be everywhere at once in their starch white uniforms trying to calm some people and medicate others.

Much like a nursing home, there is a profound feeling of unfairness. Why would one person be sane and living outside on the green grass and another be restrained in a yellow room? It was hot, and it was only May. I can't imagine a July in a place like this. The bathrooms looked uninhabitable much as they were described to me by Ginny. She had told of overflowing toilets, feces on the walls, mice, and roaches roaming around the broken tile of the floors. I could imagine that in these facilities. The bathrooms were also a victim of overuse and overcrowding. Weston was always overcrowded at one- point housing 2500 patients in a building built for 250 (Brake, 2014). Lack of care would have easily spread to the bathrooms. The kitchen and nurse's station appeared abandoned. It's difficult to imagine staff working in these rooms with water dripping from the ceiling. In some areas, the ceiling was gone, and I could see the rafters above.

I experienced the thick air of death in some rooms, and our guide assured us some patients killed themselves and each other through not in that order. Hanging seemed the most efficient way to die. Although, some patients did jump to their deaths as well. Patients died there naturally too, and are buried in a cemetery on a hill near the hospital. They were unable to escape the grounds even in death.

I could see a situation where Leo and Ginny would have had to wonder whether Tim was better off in county jail or Weston State Hospital. I am not sure how different the facilities would have been in 1980-88. There would have violence and death in both places. I guess the one benefit would have been the opportunity for Tim to get some mental health treatment while he was a patient at Weston. I am not saying that there was no attempt at positivity at Weston. I observed patient art in several forms. There was a series of masks on display. There was a project where the patients would paint the inside of the mask as they saw themselves and the outside as the patients thought others saw them. There were patient paintings and sketches. However, Weston was also known for using controversial techniques such as lobotomies, electric shock, and hydrotherapy for patients they could not control.

From the outside of the grounds of Weston State Hospital, the green and saggy maple trees show the absolute beauty of life. The green rolling hills of West Virginia lie quietly in the background. The stone buildings are regal. The water fountain is cleaning. I am just not sure how that looks from the inside of the barred windows of the small, decrepit rooms. I looked out many of the windows today. The outside seemed miles away like a painting I wanted to step into but could not. The guide pointed out that if one looked at the windows straight on the bars on the window couldn't be seen. I noticed that if one looked at the windows from any other angle, all one could see is bars.

The Trans-Allegheny Lunatic Asylum (which later become Weston State Hospital) was a psychiatric hospital that was operated from 1864 until 1994 by the state of West Virginia in the city of Weston, West Virginia (Gleason, 2014). The hospital became Weston State hospital in 1913, and it was changed back to its original name after it re-opened as a tourist attraction. The hospital offers paid tours (Brake, 2014). Built by the architect, Richard Andres, it was constructed from 1858-1881. It was initially designed to house 250 patients. It became overcrowded in the 1950's and at one point (the 1950's) had 2,500 patients (Brake, 2014).

The main hospital building is claimed to be one of the largest hand-cut stone masonry buildings in the United States, and the second largest sandstone building in the world (Brake, 2014). The largest is the Moscow Kremlin (Brake, 2014). The hospital was designated a National Historic Landmark in 1990 (Gleason, 2014). It was purchased in 2007 by Joe Jordon who uses paid tours for restoration funding (Brake, 2014). In addition to the over-crowding issues, Weston State Hospital was known to use methods such as blood-letting and the hospital would put unruly patients in cages (naked) and stack them in the halls (Brake, 2014).

At the time Tim lived at Weston, the conditions were horrible. The building was over capacity, and the infrastructure was crumbling. In 1985, a Charleston, WV newspaper reported that the hospital was dirty and unkept (Gazette Mail, 1985). Patients were confined to dirty wards and bathrooms smeared with feces (Gazette Mail, 1985). Murders and Suicides continued to be reported casting an even greater shadow on the hospital and staff. In 1992 (four years after Tim was released) a male patient went missing. He wasn't found for eight days in the hospital. His decomposing body was in such bad shape that the medical examiner ruled his death as a suicide because he or she could not come up with a cause of death (Brake, 2014).

Some photos of Weston State Hospital

Photo Cred., Kimberli Roessing-Anderson, 2018

In June of 1984, Weston State Hospital turned off their air conditioning window units (approximately 87) to help with a budget shortfall. Three patients died, and two were directly attributed to the heat which was over 90 degrees in some rooms over several days. After the patients died, the director at Weston immediately turned the units back on in all of the affected areas. The rooms that had these window units were common area rooms where patients congregated during the day. These were rooms that got afternoon sun. None of the patient rooms had air conditioning in the 120-year-old hospital. Newspapers in West Virginia and across the country reported the incident (Gazette Mail, 1984). Tim would have been there during this time unless he was in the Monongalia County Jail.

In 1989, a year after Tim's release, Weston State Hospital issued new involuntary commitment rules. Remember, Tim had to be commitment by civil order. Because he had been acquitted by the WV Supreme Court, criminal commitment for the shooting was not possible. As of 1989, the admission procedure was as follows:

1. Application is made to the Circuit court by an individual who has witnessed behavior indicating that the prospective patient is likely to cause harm to himself or others and the applicant believes that these behaviors are due to mental illness, retardation, or addiction.

2. The community mental health center is contacted and ordered to determine if alternative service is available that will prevent hospitalization.

3. The prospective patient is then examined and interviewed by a licensed psychiatrist, psychologist, or physician who determines if the person fits criteria for involuntary commitment to a mental health facility.

4. Once the certification is completed, a mental health hearing is held in front of a magistrate, mental hygiene commissioner or circuit judge of the county of which the individual is a residence.

The individual must be present and represented by counsel.

5. Presiding judge/mental hygiene commissioner /magistrate will enter an order based on the evidence presented as to whether probable cause has been found.

6. If probable cause has been found, then the individual will be transported to the designated mental health facility.

7. Within ten days of admission, the physician of record will make a decision as to whether or not a final commitment application will proceed.

8. Recommendation for final commitment may be for a temporary observation period of up to six months or for an indeterminate period of commitment of up to two years. If a patient received either type of commitment, it does not mean they will be in a mental health facility for that time but that the facility/patient will not

necessarily have to return to the court during that period of time.

9. If the physician decides not to make an application for commitment, then the client may be allowed to sign voluntarily or will be discharged with appropriate planning.

Tim was committed for a period of two years after his conviction was overturned in 1986. Prior to his conviction, Tim had been housed on the Forensics Unit at Weston State Hospital. After his conviction was overturned, he may have been moved to the last remaining open ward at Weston which would have had less security and more freedom for Tim. At the end of that period, he was released to his parents as they made-arrangements for outpatient care with the Veteran's Administration. Weston had to work with a liaison from the VA.

The Forensics Ward at Weston State Hospital

Photo Cred. Kimberli Roessing-Anderson, 2018

15 TESTIMONY

The testimony of Robert (Bob) Coffman, who was the owner and sometimes bartender at Finnerty's) was short and sweet. He was a substitute teacher at the time of the trial. He knew Alan Antonek. Alan restocked his cigarette machine weekly. Bob indicated that he owned the bar that was located at 2017 University Avenue. Bob recalled the night in question because he was tending bar. He stated that the bar was not very crowded. Bob said that Alan had been there on August 1st with two friends. Bob said that he could recognize Alan on sight. He remembered that Alan was sitting at the bar talking with Tim that night. He remembered the conversation getting a little "heated" between Alan and Tim. He heard only words or phrases such as "some trouble" and "truck". Bob stated that he glared at them while he was pouring a beer. Bob said that Alan gave him a funny look. Bob Coffman pointed out Tim in the courtroom.

Mark stated that he was 23-years-old and lived in Kent, Ohio. Mark said that he was an accountant. He was Tim's brother, and the age difference was eight years. Mark was nine or ten when Tim went into the Marines. *I noticed that one of the questions asked is: Have you had any contact afterward. Well, you see after you get older you have your own problems and your own things you have to do and you see Tim is eight years older than I and thirteen years-older that my brother, so he had his own things to do through peer pressure at school, yet he always had time for Jeff and I. Whenever my mom and dad would leave or anything, Tim would always volunteer to babysit. He didn't have to be asked. I broke my leg in the fourth grade, and Tim spent the night with me at the hospital. I was in a wheelchair for quite some time, and I had to have a tutor and Tim always helped me with the tutor because I really didn't understand her. Tim never got mad at any of us. Tim was always there when we needed him. He was always somebody to talk to, and he always helped us. He took us wherever we went. He obviously was proud of us and loved us. Tim brought people home to meet us.* Mark indicated that he saw Tim on leave from the Marines and he saw Tim after he come home from the Marines. He stated that when Tim was at WVU, he would come home on the weekend or on every other weekend. When asked if Tim had changed, Mark stated that Tim tended to be by himself. Tim wasn't as open or relaxed. *Tim was tense, uptight and he always seemed to be worried. Before Tim got sick, he was a solid individual.*

The next person to testify was Rita (Tim's sister). She stated her name as Rita Chandler or Rita McWilliams. *There is a two -year age difference. I was a sophomore when Tim was a senior. Because of our closeness in age, we were probably closer than the other boys. We spent lots of time together. We spent summers together with our grandparents in Mannington on the farm, of course. We also went to Petersburg where we have a camp on the river and we fished and swam.* Rita indicated that they grew up together. Tim was her big brother and protective of her. Rita said that Tim was a super person. Tim was a very healthy intelligent person.

Rita indicated that it was hard for her to follow in Tim's footsteps being two years behind him in school. They had the same teachers, and it set a tough path for her. He was captain of the football team. Rita stated that Tim had dated one of her friends, Julia ███████ She was a majorette. *Tim was popular, well-liked, and he gave me a lot of guidance as big brothers do.* Rita said that if Tim thought she was hanging around with the wrong people, he would take me out on the back porch and tell me so. Rita thought they were pretty close.

Tim's Senior Picture from 1971

Courtesy Buckhannon Upshur High School, 2018

When Rita was asked about Tim's time in the Marine Corps, she testified: *We wrote for some and sent postcards and that I got to know a little bit about Saudi Arabia and Tunisia and things Tim did over there and the weird things that went on. I would see Tim when he was on leave. In 1975, he would come and visit, and he would want to see my baby. Tim went hunting with my husband. Tim was fine. After Tim enrolled at WVU in January of 1976, we talked on the phone, and he visited me on weekends. I did have my own family and people do grow apart. Tim called me because we were close. I was one of the only people he could trust. Tim spoke to me about the military as things started to get worse. I knew that he was a security guard and that he had a sharp-shooting medal. Tim used to talk about being a security guard. He would lock-up and walked through the embassy at night. One night while securing the building, he came across some secret papers he wasn't supposed to see.*

Tim started calling Rita at night, and he would be crying. She knew he needed help, but she didn't know what to do to help him. Rita stated that Tim changed while he was in the Middle East, but it wasn't that bad at first. He wasn't the huge, good-looking man that she knew before he went into the service. *Tim was thinner and everything when he came back, but he seemed alright. Tim had a girlfriend, and we all figured he would marry her and all of that.* At first, Rita couldn't remember Judy's last name, but then Tim's attorney reminded her that it was Ricker. Rita indicated that she had her number and that her family was from Seattle, WA and she lived in California when she finally tracked her down when all of this happened. Rita stated that when Tim in the service, he lived with Judy in a hut over in Tunisia. Tim would write to Rita about Judy.

Tim and Judy used to go camping together on this island and all kinds of stuff like that, but he sent Judy home to meet the family one summer. I believe it was, and that led us to believe that they would get married. Tim had never done that before. Judy spent the summer with them. Tim would always write me about how fine they were getting along and everything, and when Tim came back and he enrolled in the university and what he told me was that Judy was going to get a job and help Tim through school and everything and I saw Judy after that. Judy and her sister came to my parents' house, which they are identical practically, or close to it. They were blonde and about my size or a little bigger.

The attorney asked Rita if Judy had ever gotten married and moved away. Rita indicated that she found out while Tim was at her house one time. *She had moved away and been married about two or three months. Judy did secretarial work for the government, and that is how Tim met her. After Tim returned from the military, he visited me about once a month. He enjoyed seeing the kids. Then it got so he thought everyone was against him. Tim would not eat at my parent's house because he thought my mother was trying to poison him. I would try to feed him because he looked malnutricious. Tim always ate health food stuff. When I visited him in Morgantown, he had all of this sea algae and stuff around and fruits and stuff. He had a lot of fruit, but he didn't have any money.*

When asked if there was ever a time that Rita stopped believing stories that Tim was telling her, Rita indicated that it got worse with time. Rita described bodies being carried through the embassy in mail sacks. She said she had no reason to believe this would not happen. There was one story in particular that made Rita believe that Tim was hallucinating. He said that he was babysitting for real good friends. *He was keeping their baby one night when he put on the headphones to the stereo and this voice came on and told him to throw (redacted) whatever was in his hands (Tim had just picked up the baby). Tim threw the baby across the room killing it. Tim said the government came in and took his good friends away. They were husband and wife and Tim never saw them again.* That is when Rita began disbelieving him.

Rita stated that when Tim told the story, he was sitting in her kitchen and crying. Rita believed that Tim believed that it was true. Tim also believed that he had been sent to Washington to be deprogrammed. *Tim said that the government gave him drugs to forget what he had seen and done in Tunisia and Saudi Arabia in the service at the embassies.* Tim would call Rita late at night (her husband worked the night shift) crying. He once asked her if Kathryn William's daughter had been raped, which had not happened. Kathryn Williams was a family friend. He also called one night and said that people were following him and that his phone was bugged. Tim said that he couldn't talk to Rita for long because he felt like people were watching him and following him.

Tim had told Rita that if anything happened to him, he was writing down names and he had pictures and they would be under the coffee table. One person was Judy; one was a guy he knew in the service, one was a former professor and one of them Rita did not know. Tim had told her to immediately go to his apartment and get them. Rita said she was supposed to contact these people because they would know what happened to Tim. Rita and her mother went to Tim's apartment after the police search and found the photos and names of Tim's friends. Rita stated the whole thing didn't make sense. Rita said that she had spoken to Tim two weeks before the shooting. Tim had just popped in around 2 or 3 pm. He asked again about Kathryn's daughter being raped and Tim asked if I had had been raped. Tim admitted that something was wrong with him. He thought that the drugs he had been given were wearing off and he was starting to remember just bits and pieces and it was driving him crazy. Tim didn't know what was real and what was not real. Rita stated that she asked Tim to get some help. The last thing that Tim said to Rita was, *"You think I am crazy too."*

On Cross-examination, Rita explained that she had moved to Cleveland in the last year. Rita got married when she was a junior in high school and that she and Tim had grown apart some after he went into the service and she started her own family. Rita admitted that Tim talked about other things when he came to her house. He talked about school and friends and was able to get off the topic of the military and hold a normal conversation. Rita explained that he could carry on a conversation, but would sometimes fall into a daze and stare right at you. Tim would come and go in a conversation. When asked about Tim's health food, Rita said that Tim was legally blind without his glasses and that Tim thought the health food would restore his sight. Tim also thought all of the vitamins might help his brain remember things. When asked when Judy got married, Rita said that she could only speculate. She figured it was 1976 or 1977 and that Judy was not married long. She was divorced and she and Tim were writing letters back and forth to each other.

Tim's mother (Ginny) took the stand and said that she had resided in Buckhannon, WV since 1964. Before that, they lived in Clarksburg, WV. She said that she was a substitute aid in the school system and that she had been doing that for two years. She described her husband's work history and then listed her children (Tim, Rita, Mark, and Jeff). Ginny stated that Jeff was in the courtroom. Jeff was acknowledged. Tim's attorney stated that Jeff would have only been five or six when Tim went into the Marines. Tim's mother was asked to described Tim's life up and to the point that he went into the Marines. She stated that of all of her kids, Tim was the most dependable. Ginny testified that Tim was quiet and was often to himself and that he helped the other children.

Tim entertained himself and as he got older, he became interested in fishing, hunting, and outdoor sports. Tim went caving his senior year. He wasn't very good about going to friend's houses to stay the night but that our house was often full especially at mealtime. I never had any trouble with Tim. I didn't worry about him when he was out because he was dependable. He had girlfriends and sometimes two dates for dances and proms. Tim was smart and if he were asked a question and didn't know the answer, he would go and look it up in the encyclopedia. Tim's grades were above average. He loved football. Tim's stature was much bigger that it is in court. His neck and arms were bigger because he was in a weight problem. Tim ran track and was also in a weight program with a friend at Wesleyan.

Ginny stated that Tim was president of the Athletic Club and the Varsity Club. Tim was a class officer, on the homecoming court, and an escort for the Strawberry Festival. Tim also volunteered washing pots and pans at a food center. Tim's attorney talked about how we all change after high school. He entered Tim's yearbook into evidence and displayed his senior picture to the jury. Tim's mother agreed that Tim had changed in appearance. He was not as big and bulky as he had been when he played sports.

Tim had wanted to go to college since the first grade. He didn't want to put the burden on us. Tim was very independent. Tim had odd jobs and always had his own spending money. Tim decided to go into the Marines to pay for college. Tim did his basic training at Parris Island and then he was shipped to Camp LeJeune. At some point, Tim was bored and volunteered to go overseas. Tim took an officer's training course and then he went to Embassy Security School. Tim was first assigned to Saudi Arabia. This was considered a hardship, so he was only there for year. Tim then went to Tunisia. Tim was there over a year.

The attorney for Tim showed his mother a copy of Tim's military records. It was Defendant's Collective Exhibit No. 8 which contained sixteen sheets. The entry date was March 11, 1971, and the years obligated were six. There would be four years of active duty and two years of reserve. March 31, 1971, to November of 1975 and then reserve duty. On August 27, 1973, Tim was granted final top-secret clearance. Some of the records were filled with remarks regarding Tim's performance. One stated that Tim was mature, intelligent, trustworthy, a noncommissioned officer. There was a certificate for good conduct. On June 6, 1973, his completion of security guard school was complete. He was 9th out of 110 students.

Ginny testified that when Tim was stationed in the states, he came home on holidays and leave. When Tim was out of the country, he had no leave. Tim did not see his family for the two years while overseas. She said that as soon as Tim got home, he went immediately to Morgantown, WV to enroll in school and find an apartment. He moved into 44 Jones Ave. He lived there the entire time he was a student. Ginny stated that Tim visited when he had time. Ginny testified that sometimes she and Rita would visit Tim in Morgantown during the day when Tim had time. She indicated that Tim had changed.

Tim didn't talk much. In the year before the shooting, he didn't joke and talk with me like he used to do. Tim always seemed to be afraid of something. I would lose him in conversation. Tim would just stare off. He was worried that we didn't keep the doors locked at the house. He would wait for Mark and Jeff to get home and then lock-up the house. I wasn't aware that Tim thought I was trying to poison him but I suspected it because he wasn't eating my homemade meals, my canned food, and he didn't come home for Christmas the last year before the shooting. Tim said that he got the days confused and didn't come home until the day after Christmas.

On cross-examination, Ginny was questioned about how much Tim kept to himself during his childhood. She stated that he entertained himself. She said that he had friends that came over but didn't have to have all that noise all the time and that Tim didn't like noise. When asked about the reserve time that Tim was supposed to serve, she said that she did not think he went to meetings or any camps. She did not know if he had fulfilled his commitment to the reserves. When asked about visiting Tim during the four years at WVU, she said that she did. She visited him and he visited the family in Buckhannon. The prosecutor made the point that Tim was capable of having normal conversations and his mother said that he could but sometimes she would lose him. Ginny was asked if she was alarmed by Tim's behavior, she stated that she was because he was afraid all of the time.

However, she admitted that she had not taken him to a doctor or suggest that he see a doctor. She also admitted that Tim had never threatened anyone. Tim's mother stated she could not remember the last time she saw her son before the shooting but that she had seen him sometime during the summer. Finally, the prosecutor asked her if her husband would have gone to see Tim without her and she stated that he would not.

There was a redirect. Tim's mother was asked about the condition of his apartment on her last visit. The usually very neat Tim was neglecting everything. *He usually took special care in his appearance, room and things clean. Everything was a mess and that there were signs everywhere reminding him to take certain things for his health.* She stated that there was a sign for Zinc for his eyes. Ginny could not ever remember seeing Tim's apartment in this condition.

Leo testified that he was a teacher in machine trades at the Tri-County Vocational Tech Center in Buckhannon. He had been a teacher for fourteen years. He explained his job and how he got there as a machinist. He had been a machinist after graduating from Washington Irving High School in 1951. He testified that he had taken a job at Moore Business Forum and moved the family to Buckhannon. Leo was then asked about the relationship he had with Tim as he was growing up.

I was closer to Tim than any of the other children probably because he was the oldest child. I expected more from Tim and they were close despite the fact that I sometimes worked double shifts. I got Tim an English Bulldog (Princess) for Christmas one year. I used my vacation pay to buy it for him when he was three or four- years-old. I took Tim to sign up for Pop Warner Football. Tim loved football and he got that from me. Every Friday I took the old fishing truck and went to Spruce Knob Lake or down to the Cabin at Petersburg to fish. Mother didn't approve of these trips but she put up with it because we were pretty close. I did more with Tim than any of my other children.

Leo stated that Tim was a good student and that he was 26th or 27th within a class of 300 students. He said that Tim excelled. There were never in any problems with Tim. Leo stated that Tim was not a violent person. Leo was always proud of him. Leo talked about Tim coming home on leave. He also stated that he did not see Tim for 27 months. Leo stated that the government kept Tim for an extra three months with no explanation. *It was at the convenience of the government.* Three photos of Tim were introduced after a discussion of Tim's changed appearance. One was marked "Promotion Day," and that was the day that Tim became a sergeant.

Leo stated (when asked about Judy) that Tim had written his mother and asked for Judy to come and visit one summer and she stayed for three months. Leo said that she came from Tunisia but she was an American. He said she was in California. *I had an address for her from four years ago, but they had not been able to find her in the weeks before the trial. Judy was a secretary for the government, but she was the kind of person that could be in Saudi Arabia one day and California the next.* Leo stated that he never understood that. Leo said that Tim was not home when Judy visited that summer. The family toured West Virginia with Judy that summer. They took her to the Cass Railroad one weekend for example. Leo did not know where Judy went we she left their house. She did come back to the house with Tim when he was discharged. Leo stated that she and Tim went to Bethesda, MD which normally only takes one day for a discharge but in Tim's case it took three days. Leo testified that he tried to find out why it took three days, but he could not get any answers. Leo also stated that when Tim went to WVU, Judy went to California. Leo tried to testify to something that Judy told him in their kitchen in Buckhannon after Tim was discharged, but the prosecution objected. Hearsay. Neither the prosecution nor the defense could find Judy for trial (according to trial transcripts). The judge would not allow the testimony. I asked Judy about this statement when I interviewed her, but she did not remember the conversation with Leo.

Leo testified about his relationship with Tim while Tim was attending WVU. He had noticed that Tim was always carrying a gun or had one in his car. Leo stated that he told Tim that guns will get you into trouble, but that Tim seemed afraid of something. Leo admitted that he and Jeff visited Tim in the two weeks before the shooting when Jeff was in Morgantown for a swim meet. He said that his wife wasn't with him. Leo had taken Tim to Fish & Chips to eat on the far side of Morgantown. Leo stated that he always asked Tim if he needed anything and how he was getting along. Tim would always say that he didn't need anything and how he was fine when in fact his grades were slipping, he was dropping classes, and failing subjects. Leo admitted that Rita did tell him about Tim's odd behavior, but that it didn't make any sense to him.

During cross- examination, Leo said that he had asked Tim to come home with him for the weekend while he was visiting with Jeff, but Tim had said that he had things to do. Leo was presented with prior testimony about the visit being the last Saturday of July and he said that it could have been. He stated that they had a normal conversation, but he did get on Tim about the condition of his apartment. *It looked like a dump.*

There was a powerful parade of witnesses that came in to speak on Tim's behalf. There were teachers that testified about what a great student Tim was in high school. They talked about how intelligent Tim was and how much promise he encompassed. Teachers said he was mature and serious about going to college and becoming an engineer. There were friends that spoke to what a dependable friend Tim could be and how he would help anyone in need. Former coaches came forward to praise Tim as both an athlete and a leader. He was a coach's dream because he was coachable and Tim had a great attitude. Tim was a co-captain of the football team in high school, and he was held in high regard by everyone. His former high school counselor became emotional on the stand when talking about Tim and how much promise he had shown.

On cross-examination, the prosecution asked each one of these witnesses how much contact they had with Tim since he went into the military. The answer was almost always the same. Aside from his high school counselor, no one had any meaningful contact with Tim since late summer of 1971. He had visited with a few friends when he came home on leave from Camp Lejeune, but none had spoken with him since he came back from Tunisia and enrolled at WVU in the Mining Engineering Department. The school counselor was the only person he had contacted, and it was just the one time.

I believe even the jury in the second trial realized that the Tim on trial with the bushy beard and large glasses was not the same Tim that shined at Buckhannon Upshur High School. This may have been why after he was convicted, the jury asked for mercy for Tim. Most people realized that something had happened to Tim and that he was mentally ill. The people that testified for Tim at trial didn't know the Tim in the courtroom, and one former friend from junior high school (Michael Ward) testified that he had to have Tim pointed out to him at the defense table. He didn't even recognize Tim.

16 BACK TO MORGANTOWN

I was sitting on the porch of the family's cabin near Winter Park, Colorado in July when my cell-phone rang. Hummingbirds were buzzing by my head, and I almost didn't answer so as not to scare them. It was the Monongalia County Records Department. When I had been there in May, I had looked at thousands of pages of documents, made over 100 copies, and filled two large legal pads with notes. However, I had been told that the trial exhibits were gone. There had been a move from an old courthouse to a new courthouse, and the exhibits from this trial didn't make the trip. I had also been told that often lawyers take the exhibits back after the trial. I doubted that Tim's lawyer had done this since he appealed the case.

After I came back to Denver in May, I filed an additional West Virginia FIOA for just the exhibits on the off chance that someone might look for them. The woman from the courthouse in Monongalia County was calling to say that she had gone to the basement of the old Monongalia County Courthouse and found some of the exhibits. She said she didn't have it all, but she had a couple of boxes. I thought about it for a few days, and I decided to return to Morgantown to go through the boxes. I went back in August. It was worth it. To see the crime scene photos, the photos of Tim's basement apartment three days after the crime, to go through his yearbook and read the comments, and to handle the shells and bullets made a massive difference in the writing of this book. I was able to develop a much more coherent picture of Tim's life at WVU.

Looking at Tim's life through the evidence boxes was less like looking through a microscope and more like looking through a Kila descope. All of the designs were made of red shotgun shells.

I decided to make an appointment to go through the stacks at The Dominion Post and do some research at the

Morgantown Library as well. One of the items I had been trying to get was Tim's military records. The records were with the exhibits. The records glowed with recommendations and comments of his character. Tim was in stellar shape, and except for a smallpox scar had not a mark on his body when he enlisted. I ran my hands over the yearbook and read all of the comments. I had found the yearbook online but this was Tim's off-white discolored leather yearbook, and it gave some insight into how others felt about him in 1971. Tim was well-liked by his classmates and teachers. It's a small world. Imagine my surprise when I noticed my father's cousin's (George Roessing) signature in Tim's yearbook. They knew each other in 1971 when I was four-years-old and 14 years before I would ever meet Jeff.

I held the bullets in my hands. They were in small manila envelopes, and I poured them out onto the desk. They were cold and misshapen. I wondered how such small pieces of metal could do so much damage. I looked at the chalk outline of Alan's body on the sidewalk, and thought how could a 19-year-old young man be reduced to this? At midnight, Alan was alive and drinking a beer. He was watching a girl sing and play guitar. At 1a.m. Alan was dead on the Stadium Bridge in Morgantown. It was hard for me to grasp.

Finnerty's Bar had been closed for years. I was holding photos of the outside and the inside of the bar. I had not been able to reach Bob Coffman during the research phase of the book and so I had no idea what Finnerty's looked like in 1980. It was not what I had imagined. It was smaller and had all of the décor that the late 70's could muster. The pictures were dark. The photographer should have used a flash. They were black and white. The police had asked Bob Coffman to re-enact Tim's movements from the night of the shootings. Bob Coffman, his wife (Priscilla) and a few unidentified people are in the photos. It was a window into that night in four photographs. The walls were covered in paneling. Every few feet found an ashtray.

The bar stools looked like they had red leather tops but it was difficult to tell in a black and white photo. There were tables and chairs. There were no pictures of the game room. Bob Coffman looked the part with the 70's hair and beard. His tee-shirt was tight. Someone had on bell-bottom jeans that were frayed. A few men had on very short shorts (I guess that was the style at the time). Shelves filled with liquor stood behind the bar. A dark-haired woman with a Billy-Jean-King style haircut was bartending. From the outside, Finnerty's could be missed in the blink of an eye. A small white vertical sign with a *Enjoy Coca Cola* sign below it. It was stuffed between a pizza den and another bar. It crossed my mind that Tim could have stopped in any of the places. There was a bar or restaurant every few feet. If Tim had stopped at any one of those other places, the shooting might not have happened.

The evidence boxes also contained photos of Tim as a Marine. He is with fellow marines in one color photo and he looks quite serious. His huge black glasses overwhelm his face. Tim always looked serious and I am not sure that I ever saw him smile. There are a couple of photos of Tim on a beach and still no smile. I went back through every photo of Tim I have seen (all the way back to the 9th grade) and there are no smiles. I also went back through my memory and no smiles. I did see him chuckle to himself a few times, but he would cover his mouth with his hand.

The photos of Tim from the evidence box and The Record Delta looked more like the man I knew. Minus the mustache and long beard, this was the Tim I broke bread with and played cards against in 1987 and 1988. The senior picture of Tim that hung behind the couch on Victoria Street was foreign to me. I didn't know the Tim with the confident look, the handsome face and the bleach blonde hair. He was a stranger to me. He may have been a stranger to Tim too.

17 VICTORIA STREET

March 8, 2018, would have been a cool morning in
Buckhannon. There was some snow on the ground. At 6 a.m.,
people would have been starting to turn on lights and turn off
alarm clocks. Some would be hitting the snooze button a
couple of times. It was a Thursday, and people were eyeing
the weekend. The smell of coffee and a lit fireplace would
have filled the noses of those wandering toward their
bathrooms to shower. On Victoria Street, something different
was happening. The final act of a long drama was unfolding,
and it was violent. This wasn't a scene for the faint of heart.

An 84-year-old Leo McWilliams had climbed the steep
stairs to the attic bedroom were Tim had slept when I knew
him. A fight had ensued between them. A fight between the

two would not have been noiseless. Ginny would have been up wondering what was happening above her. At some point, Tim climbed on his father's back, lifted his head by the hair, and slit Leo's throat. Blood would have filled the floor and Leo would have gasped for life. Tim had a stab wound to the forearm. Did Leo stab him? Did Tim stab himself? According to the chief medical examiner (Allen Mock), Leo would have died with seconds or minutes.

Ginny called 911 for help. She told the 911 operator that her son had a stab wound to the arm. First responders found Leo deceased upstairs and asked for police assistance. Tim was taken to St. Joseph's Hospital. He was treated and released into the custody of law enforcement. Leo was driven to the medical examiner's office in Charleston, WV. Ginny had been downstairs during the incident according to police sources. While many in Buckhannon were eating breakfast, flipping on the news, and warming their cars, the McWilliams' family had already lived a day of tragedy. Tim was arrested for his father's murder after he was released from the hospital.

A day later, one in which I am sure was filled with panicked phone calls, tears, grief, and arranging travel, the family made their first public comments about "Standing by Tim". The family believed that he may have acted in self-defense. According to the family, Leo suffered from both Alzheimer's Disease and dementia. One of Leo's sons (either Mark or Jeff) made this comment to the press from the house on Victoria Street. The medical examiner did not list either of these conditions as contributing factors to Leo's death. When interviewed by authorities, Tim said that he got into a fight with his dad. He told authorities that he got onto Leo's back and cut his throat with a knife. According to Sheriff David Coffman, Tim was charged with murder and transported to the Tygart Valley Regional Jail. He is being held without bond after his initial appearance before Magistrate John Michael Coffman (no relation). Deputy Seth Cutright confirmed that the men shared a home.

According to Cutright, Tim was Mirandized, and he then gave a statement. Cutright is the lead investigator in the case. The criminal complaint filed by Deputy Cutright gives few details not listed in the initial press release. Ginny called 911 first, and the EMS called for the police after finding Leo's body. The complaint blacks out Tim's social security number and a driver's license number which leads me to believe that Tim had a driver's license. This would be one of the first indications that he had any public record since he was released from Weston State Hospital in the late 1980's.

By April 20, 2018, The Charleston Gazette finally broke the story that included Tim's past. The journalist used the 1986 Supreme Court decision easily accessible online. The Record Delta followed. I received the case numbers after filing a West Virginia FOIA at some point in between. The preliminary hearing that had been scheduled for March 19th was postponed. Tim's attorney has the same last name as Mark's wife (Willet). Willet was her maiden name. He stated that Tim would undergo a mental evaluation before the hearing. Willet stated to the press that Tim had not fully recovered from his mental illness. He indicated that since this is a capital case, a competency evaluation needs to be completed. Both Judge Kurt Hall and the prosecutor (David Godwin) agreed.

On May 3, 2018, Circuit Judge Hall ordered Tim to undergo a competency evaluation. Godwin had no objection, and the judge granted the motion to have a forensic psychologist, Dr. William Fremouw, conduct the interview regarding Tim's competency and criminal responsibility. Godwin stated that there would be a new grand jury in session in September of 2018.

Criminal Complaint from the stabbing on March 8, 2018

Buckhannon Upshur County, 2018

18 TIM'S HANDWRITING

Monongalia County Public Records

Upon seeing Tim's signature on some police forms, I was startled. He had the signature of a junior high school girl. It stopped me in my tracks. I made some copies of his signature and decided to do some research. I am no expert, but I did have a book on handwriting analysis, so I studied it. Notice the o's for the dot in his i's. According to my research, this is called ornamentation (Hollander, 1999). It is usually found in teenage writers, mainly girls. Ornamentation is any addition to writing that takes extra time and interrupts the natural flow. It is written by someone who is trying to attract attention to themselves. It is an indicator that the writer does not feel they are receiving attention or the right kind of attention. It is a negative indicator. It suggests that the writer feels insecure (Hollander, 1999).

The loops in the ll's also caught my eye. The loops are stress indicators. The more width in each loop, the more stress the writer is feeling. I noticed on a Miranda form where there were three signature lines; the last line had the most pressure and the widest width between the loops. Pressure being the harder the writer presses down with the instrument. This is also a stress indicator (Hollander, 1999). I had never thought much about handwriting, but his signature was so odd for what would have been a 27-year-old man that I had to examine it.

19 SCHIZOPHRENIA

The American Psychiatric Association defines schizophrenia as "a disorder consisting of delusions, hallucinations, disorganized speech, grossly disorganized/bizarre behavior and a lack of organized speech activity, or emotions (Delisi, 2017) with active symptoms for at least a month. Usually, at least two of the symptoms are present. The illness begins with a prodromal stage, and after treatment or an acute episode subsides may be in a so-called "residual" stage both having some nonspecific behavior symptoms. At least six months with continuous signs of some disturbance should be present" (DeLisi, 2017).

During this period, an individual with schizophrenia is considered impaired in his or her ability to perform at work, attend school, or participate in social activities. Schizophrenia can be diagnosed with hallucinations, delusions, disorganized speech or catatonic behavior, and negative systems. Two of these five symptoms are required, and at least one of them must be delusions, hallucinations, or disorganized speech (Delisi, 2017).

While researching schizophrenia, I discovered that almost anything could be listed as a possible cause, much like cancer. The trial transcripts indicated that there was heavy use of marijuana and alcohol in the year leading up to the shooting. Tim was also a winter baby in 1953. Some statistics indicate that babies born in the winter have a higher chance of developing schizophrenia because their mothers may have contracted influenza in the first half of pregnancy (Schizophrenia, 20014). It is more common in males (Delisi, 2017). There is also the possibility of a genetic transfer (Delisi, 2017). While much more is known about schizophrenia now than in 1980, much is still to be learned.

Tim's schizophrenia seemed to develop when he came home from Tunisia and started college at WVU. He was isolated and lonely. His structure had changed. Tim complained of being unable to concentrate on a summer course in 1978. His family testified at trial that he would often stare off during conversations and some doctors believed that Tim suffered from Petit Mal seizures. This is an older term for absence seizures which cause a person to stare off into space or blank out for a short period. Like other seizures, they are caused by a brief abnormal electrical activity in a person's brain (Delisi, 2017).

Tim was evaluated by a plethora of doctors from 1980-1988 and beyond. Many agreed that Tim understood the basics. He knew what court was and what lawyers do. He knew what the job of the jury was and he was able to answer questions correctly about the date, time, and the day of the week. He could have lucid conversations about family and sports. He could talk about his friends from high school. The differences in opinion came when different doctors tried to decide whether or not Tim was sane at the time of the shootings in 1980. While some doctors were unbiased, others worked for either the defense or the prosecution. Their decisions would determine if Tim would stand trial for the shootings.

Some of what came out during this 8-year-period of examination would be that Tim was deeply afraid of something. He was afraid when an Egyptian student moved into the building behind his apartment. He was afraid of what he termed, "Arabs." Tim was obsessed with health food because he believed that distilled water and vitamins would regenerate his brain. Tim started running. Tim thought running made his brain think faster. He believed he had been brainwashed and that the military had used lasers to hemorrhage his brain. Tim began to break down at school over his grades.

Tim felt extremely bad about his lack of success. He began experiencing confusing thoughts about his military experiences, and he was unsure if these events had happened. He believed he had killed trespassers at the embassy in Saudi Arabia. He worried about spies, a Treasury Department Task Force and blackmail. Tim failed the same surveying class two summers in a row, his grades dropped, he dropped classes, took a semester off from school, and according to his doctors, Tim's life maintenance was destroyed. Tim began to see threats everywhere.

Tim owned a shotgun, but he purchased a .38 pistol and then a .45 pistol as his delusions increased. He began sleeping in his bathtub. Tim told his doctors that his bathtub was bulletproof and that it was worth the misdemeanor charge he could have faced for carrying a handgun. He also told doctors that his dad had warned him about carrying a gun. Tim's delusional state kept him afraid and in need of protection. Even before he shot a dog in 1978, he had shot furniture in his apartment. He once shot his mattress because he believed someone was in his bedroom. Tim was known to call the police and complain that there were prowlers. He turned on the bright blinding spotlights in his yard at night.

Newspapers at the time published the more salacious aspects of the case such as Tim's claims that the government forced him to have sexual relations with two orangutans. Tim stated that they were fed peanuts and bananas by the CIA. This was done to use as blackmail against Tim if he ever revealed top secret information. Tim also claimed that the government decapitated him, put his head on a silver platter on ice. Tim said that Gothards (a made-up word) was hung around his neck, and he was strangulated. He then stated that his head was sewn back on. He stated he could never testify because it would violate the "National Security Act." He was so frightened by this that he never spoke (even to his attorneys) during the first trial.

While he portrayed the government, CIA, and military as doing all of these things to him, he always saw them as his only hope. The same people that drugged him injected him and blackmailed him were going to burst into courtroom at the last minute with a top -secret document that would save him. He wanted his trial moved closer to Washington, DC so he would be closer to the federal government. Tim wanted to be cared for in a VA facility because they would have access to secret documents that would help him.

For Tim, this all started when he looked down at a tear in his pants one day (in 1978) and noticed a boil. He believed this was an injection site. Tim believed he had been injected with a drug to erase his memory. Tim also thought that the government checked in on him from time to time to see if he remembered things. Tim reached out twice from 1976-1980 that we know of; once was to Rita (who did not know what to do (and she told Leo). Tim also reached out school counselor.

162

He sat in this man's driveway for an hour and told him everything and that he was afraid. Cornelius C. Albaugh. served in the military for twenty years. He was Tim's guidance counselor in high school. He testified that Tim was a class leader. Albaugh stated that Tim was one the finest young man he had ever known. He said that Tim chose to go into the Marines because that was his desire. Albaugh wrote to Tim's commanding officer to help him along. Tim asked to come over to Albaugh's house in the fall of 1979. Tim explained that he needed to speak with him. They talked for an hour. Tim was very troubled. Agitated. Tim stated that the military had removed privileged information from his memory. The government had injected Tim with drugs to eliminate his memory. Tim said that all of this affected him deeply.

We do not know what the counselor did with that information. What makes this story all the sadder is that Tim knew there was something wrong and he didn't know how to get help.

I was perplexed by the school counselor. He had been a source of comfort to Tim in high school and a reference for him in the marine corp. He had glowing recommendations for Tim. He wrote a letter to Tim's commanding officer early in Tim's military career that helped him. Tim went to this man when his life was falling apart. Even though they had lost touch for a couple of years after Tim got out of the Marines and Tim enrolled at WVU, Tim turned to this counselor when he was in trouble. What did Albaugh do for him?

Tim told him about the injections, the top-secret documents, the flashbacks, and the fears. Tim told his counselor that he thought he was "going crazy." According to court testimony, the counselor believed Tim believed what he was saying. He thought that it was possible that the government was behind Tim's problems and that they might have injected him with a drug to make him forget what happened at the embassy and or secret documents.

Even after reading the testimony of this counselor and transcripts of what Tim had told his various doctors, I wasn't clear if the counselor did anything with the information Tim had entrusted to him. I don't believe Tim, and this counselor ever spoke again. I wonder if the counselor ever reached out to the family or anyone else or if Tim asked him not to say anything. I wonder if this counselor attempted to get Tim to seek further help? It just seems odd that they had this conversation in a car in a driveway for an hour and that was it.

20 SORROW

The blonde-haired, blue-eyed captain of the high school football team is now a 65-year-old greying man. The Tim that littered the pages of his high school yearbook and won over so many people during his youth is gone. Tim walked into the Marines as one person and came out the other side as someone else. He did not look the same, and his personality was forever changed. Why? We do not know. While he maintained some composure for two years at WVU, he eventually began decompensating before the eyes of all he knew, and no one knew how to help him. What happened to Timothy Allen McWilliams?

When his name is Googled, the 1986 WV Supreme Court case pops up like a Jack in the Box. The many newspapers across the country that covered his three-day trial in 1984 had left Tim behind long ago. They went on to cover all of the other shootings and killings that have happened on a daily basis in this country. After being discharged from Weston State Hospital, Tim disappeared into his parent's house. He went back to his attic bedroom where his was once a king. Tim was surrounded by sports trophies and memories of long ago. A mere shadow of himself, Tim was freed from jail and Weston, but I doubt he was ever truly free. Friends of Leo didn't even know Tim lived there. Victims and witnesses of the 1980 shooting thought he was still in a mental institution.

When I knew Tim, life was still relatively simple. People had landline phones and cable. Few people had computers, and the only cell phone (car phone) I had ever seen was on a Perry Mason Mystery Special on television. There was no internet. There were no iPods. When I last saw Tim, he was sitting at the kitchen table with Leo. Little bulldog puppies ran around his legs. That is how I remember Tim. He shuffled when he walked. Ginny had to coax Tim to speak even basic greetings. Leo interacted with him the most. Tim always looked like he was on the edge of tipping over physically and mentally.

There were many questions beyond my reach. Over the last 30 years, did Tim take his medication? Did the V.A. help him? Did Tim see a doctor on a regular basis? Did he evolve with technology? Did he visit Florida or Alabama on vacation to see his family? What did Tim do all of that time? Now when Tim's name is Googled, a plethora of articles pop up from the 1980 shooting, the WV Supreme Court case, and the stabbing from earlier this year. His anonymity is gone. If this case goes to trial, I wonder if his new attorney will dust off the 1971 yearbook and use it again to try and wow the jury even though that is not who he is or has been for a long time.

The inclination is to feel sorry for Tim and I do feel sorry for him. He was cheated out of a normal life and burdened with insanity. He got sick during a time when little was known about PTSD, and the study of schizophrenia was still developing. No one helped Tim between 1978, and 1980 and he reached out for help. Had Tim gotten help after he shot the tail off of a dog, he might not have shot three people in 1980. Hindsight is always 20/20.

Sorrow must also be felt for the family of Alan Antonek who was shot on the Stadium Bridge in Morgantown a little after midnight on August 1, 1980. He was shot after having some sort of communication with a very unstable young man in a bar. His family and friends lost a brother and a son. I am sure that they have no idea why. Alan's sister did not want to speak about the case, and I respect that decision. I am certain that she has suffered enough.

Sorrow must be felt for Michael Carter and Donald Askew who were both shot that night and their lives changed forever. They both suffered life-threatening wounds and spent time in the hospital. I spoke to Donald's brother, and he stated that Donald was doing well but didn't want to relive the case. I can't blame him. Sorrow must be felt for Leo. I know his family loved him. He was always well-liked. The fact that Leo and Ginny lived with Tim seems like a recipe for disaster. It saddens me to think of how Leo spent his last moments. He must have been terrified. Yet, I am certain that if he could have spoken last words to Tim, they would have been kind and forgiving.

Unless Tim pleads in this year's case or is found incompetent, there will be a trial in Buckhannon, West Virginia. As I write this, he is being evaluated by mental health professionals. No decision has been made on Tim's future, and he resides without bond at the Tygart Regional Jail. As sad as it is that Tim was once such a promising young man with such a bright future, it is equally sad that in some ways, those facts stood in the way of him getting help. No one wanted to be the one to stain his future opportunities and interrupt his future by labeling Tim as mentally ill. In that vain attempt to save the good-looking, homecoming court escort, talented athlete with the great grades, they lost the more dark-haired thinner young man who was failing courses in the summer of 1978. Both were gone.

21 44 JONES AVE.

It still stands. The house was not what it once was as off-white siding now covered the red brick. The outside of the house appeared neglected with only a basic attempt made to make it presentable for potential renters. The sidewalk was old and cracked. The street was filled with potholes. Litter was lying in the creases between the sidewalk and the street. The back porch has been enclosed, and the back of the house extended. There was an address on the front of the house that read 44 Jones Ave., and then a 43 ½ was spray-painted over it. The basement apartment was still there with its window into yesterday. Only the red brick of the chimney was sticking out to signal me that I had the right house. The red and white awning was long gone, and the woodwork and craftsmanship were splattered with boring brown paint. The green jungle that once protected Tim in 1980 has been cleared and replaced by gravel for a large parking lot that probably makes bank on WVU game days.

What was once a fine house was now a reminder of what used to be among much nicer accommodations for students in a college town. There was no screen or glass outer door to protect the inside from the outside or the outside from the inside. As I marveled at all of the shades of green in the front of the house in the form of plants, shrubs, and trees, I wondered if any of these trees had been there when Tim called this house, home. If only trees and flowers could speak, what a wonderful world it would be. I could imagine Tim living and breathing there in that basement apartment. I could see him looking out of the back window and standing on the porch that used to be there. I could see Tim sleeping in the bathtub.

The first photo is 44 Jones Ave. from the back where Tim lived from 1976-1980.

Photo Cred. Monongalia County Public Records

The second photo is that same place in 2018

Photo Cred. Kimberli Roessing-Anderson, 2018

Tim as a Marine in 1971

Courtesy, Monongalia County Public Records

Tim being arrested on August 3, 1980

Courtesy, The Dominion Post, 2018

Tim in court in 1984

Courtesy, The Dominion Post, 2018

Letters that Tim wrote to Judy in 1980

Monongalia County Public Records

1 July 80
2/00

Judy,
    Classes started for the second semester of summer school today, so it's 5 weeks of thermodynamics & the strength of materials. I have been getting healthy again & actually ran 38 miles last week. I had one month off & didn't do anything except relax here & run. I am eating well — whole wheat bagels from the bakery & familia which is made of oats, bran, germ, raisins & dried peaches. I also add on spoonful of brewer's yeast to each bowl. My head hurts from the running, nutrition, & vitamins and I have memories.; I firmly believe that the CIA owes me money when I graduate & that I get a job offer from Island Creek in Upshur co which will be the largest coal mine east of the Mississippi. I had an IQ of 136 when I was about 14 & in college here I have been paranoid, & still continue to have memories & it has taken me too long to graduate. I could continue but I will leave it & you can please burn this letter in your grill. It's an unbelievable story which includes invoking the National Security Act to brainwash into the USMC.
    BURN !
    I'm taking two Spanish classes next semester & will eventually buy a better radio in order to listen to Spanish broadcasts. My car is unable to pass the state's inspection & shall remain that way. I want

to take the money & vacation in South America before working. They wanted to use me as a station chief here in Morgantown to protect the proposed coal liquification plant but I refused & was brainwashed again when my contract expired.

I am becoming a good cook, I specialize in natural soaps and cereal. I tried to call several times before I had my telephone disconnected & I sent two letters — one to your old address & one to the new address — before I received your letter (indicate I sent one to your office address — you should have received two letters within the last ~~two weeks~~ two months).

Did you get your kitten & is Scott still boarding with you? I am preparing to bake a casserole of eggplant, tomato-sauce, egg, parmesan, mozzarella & millet before I go to bed & I need to meet some state.

I Love You
Mac

I am eating raw eggs in stock tartar & goats milk on the families & both contain hormones which aid brain regeneration. Our behavior was thoroughly observed by "ghouls". ~~They~~ contacted me because of "Operation Chaos" in 69. That's all that I will say.

[left margin, written vertically:] I hope that you are fine & I will write about your new situation. Love you appreciate. Please burn this letter some where.

26 July 80

Judith,

I am at Maxwell's Restaurant. Leo & the swim team (Jess) were here today & he & I went to Fish & Chips. There is barely anyone in town during the last semester of summer school. I withdrew from the last semester of summer school & I still need to make-up work in the surveying class.

I sold my car to a junkyard in lieu of making repairs or getting tickets & I am down to pennies. Deep Cover? We should be on vacation in twelve months or I will rant Marxist rhetoric & hijack a plane. I will have wasted months in USMC & 1½ years of college due to concealment or cover and petit mal & brainwash.

I am attempting to get a lot of physical therapy & my diet is whole wheat bagels, familia, raw eggs, etc. with distilled water which lowers my blood pressure so much that I travel approximately at a turtle's pace. I even bought a book on nutrition & partake of at least one teaspoon of sea algae each day. I think that if I get extremely healthy now & then quit during school that my attention span will increase.

I called 805 682 2828 several times during the evening, but there was not an answer. Is that your office & is this letter addressed to your office? I disconnected my telephone but I wish that you would write soon so that I will know your location.

This fall I need 14 hours in order to get a little small amount of money from the schools so I will take Soviet Foreign Policy & an Economics class in addition to a mining class & two classes which I have previously started & dropped which will help a little — Programming & Thermodynamics. I am tired & I feel old. USMC & 1½ years of shooting out the window & under the bed & wrecking my slightly used but old Ford.

I just had a glass of tea & the music is good so now

I will have a cup of coffee which is steaming behind the Pepsi machine while I meditate on this letter & 4 more miles. Mind over matter. Is that **Zen**? We have several Chinese students here & one Russian visitor who teaches Russian language. Detente is a long way from the Cold War. Some of us are still shooting out our windows.

Good coffee, but it's cold. The soups du jour are CLAM CHOWDER & SPLIT PEA.

I run 2.0 miles at a time. It usually requires 32:00 minutes. In Tunis I could run 3 miles in 19:30 minutes but while you were away I got into good shape.

Where is your brother? Write me a quick post card so that I'll know that you are alright.

Did you know that Mestizos & other Latin Americans who have vegetarian diets do not develope pellagra because they drink coffee which contains the essential amino acid known as tryptophan & is the equivalent of niacin in double the quantity of niacin as far as pellagra is concerned.

SeaAlgae has all of the 8 essential amino acids in a greater percentage than any other food by weight.

Helpful Trivia

I am stopping
Be Good

Love,
yo
Zim

The house on Victoria Street, 2018

Photo Cred., Kimberli Roessing-Anderson, 2018

McWilliams
West Virginia Regional Jail Authority

Monongalia County Public Record, 2018

Alan Antonek who was shot and killed on August 1, 1980

Courtesy, The Record Delta, 2018

Alan Antonek

Monongalia County Public Record from August 1, 1980

BIBLIOGRAPHY

Brake, Sherri, The Haunted History of the Trans-Alleghany Lunatic Asylum, Raven Rock, 2014, United States

The Charleston Gazette- Mail, 1980, 1984, 1985, 1986,

Delisi, MD, L., 100 Questions & Answers, Jones & Bartlett Learning, 2017, Burlington, MA

The Dominion Post, 1980, 1982, 1984,

Gleason, Edward S., Lunatic, The Rise and Fall of an American Asylum, 48-Hour Books, 2014, United States

Gilman, Charlotte Perkins, The Yellow Wallpaper, 1892, New England Magazine, United States

Hollander, P. Scott, Handwriting Analysis. A complete self-

teaching guide, Llewellyn Publications, 1999, St. Paul,

Bartlett Learning, 2017, Burlington, MA

The Record Delta, 2018

Schizophrenia linked to flu during pregnancy,

https://www.webmd.com/schizophrenia/news/200408

02/schizophrenia-linked-flu-during-pregnancy

Webster's Dictionary, 2018, New York, New York,
https://www.dictionary.com/browse/webster

West Virginia Supreme Court, State vs. McWilliams,

https://law.justia.com/cases/west-virginia/supreme-

court/1986/16821-5.html

Wikipedia,

https://www.google.com/search?source=hp&ei=JZbgW

_6oN9TTjgTE5bGYDA&q=wikipedia&oq=wiki&gs_l=

psy-ab.1.0.0i67l5j0j0i67j0l2j0i67.1121.18

Made in the USA
San Bernardino, CA
20 January 2019